# FACES OF *grief*

# FACES OF *grief*

## STORIES OF PUTTING THE PIECES BACK TOGETHER

*Samantha Ruth*

Founder of Griefhab

Cover design by Michelle Fairbanks
Published by Griefhab Books
www.Griefhab.com

ISBN: 979-8-9883184-2-2 (paperback)
ISBN: 979-8-9883184-4-6 (ebook)

Printed in the United States of America

Amy Lewis
Charles "Chic" Dabrush
Joannie Dabrush
Jackson "Skye" Dabrush-Nuesch

# GROUP DEDICATION

*C*ollectively, we dedicate this book to YOU, our readers. Whether you're navigating your own loss or supporting someone through theirs, you're taking a huge step just by reading this book. Thank you for making a difference!

This is for every individual struggling, for the families and loved ones who stand by them, and for all those who work tirelessly in the fields of mental health and grief support.

We came together to offer support in this world that often avoids grief, to remind you that you're not alone, and to assure you that you will get through this.

Your way.

At your pace.

As we strive to change the conversation and break the stigmas around grief and mental illness, we hope our stories will offer comfort, connection, and hope.

Because no one should struggle alone. Silence is the enemy.

We've got you!

And You've got this!

# IN LOVING MEMORY

Sam & Sassy
To our everything. The very best fur daddy, husband, friend, and over-all human. You are missed every second of every day, and honoring you gives us daily purpose.

Alexa Bigwarfe
In loving memory of my sweet daughter, Kathryn Matthews Bigwarfe. 12/10/11-12/12/11

Elizabeth Barbour
To two strong and loving women—Joan Trezise, my adoptive mom and Kathleen Walker, my biological mom.

Kristina Bottenberg
In loving memory of Kenzie, David and all those we love and have lost.

Brooke Carlock & Max Miller
Libby Shannon—your kindness and light live on in so many hearts. May we all strive to #LiveLikeLibby!

Bill Correll
To all the wonderful people that I have known and loved who have gone on to heaven before me, I carry you in my heart every day, I've always loved you and I always will.

Magda Hassel
My wonderful husband, thank you for our perfect love story

Tina Holmes
For all the Souls that I cared for.

Jan Jeremias
In memory of the person I was from 1962-2001

Melissa Lantto & Kailyn Tasto
In loving memory of a loving husband and father, Chris Lantto, our "Chris Kringle"

Martie McNabb
Alan C. McNabb

Carin Mikos
To my grandparents Mildred and Ernest Mikos and Mildred and Conrad Erickson. Thank you for your wisdom and your love.

Danielle Miller
Live for today because tomorrow is never promised!

Kate Mollison
Craig, thank you for teaching me what love feels like. I'm honored to have been your soul mate. Love you 3,000. Forever, your Mrs. Mollison

Dan Older
Brad Older

Charity Pimentel-Hyams
Your shoes were ridiculously large and impossible to fill. In loving memory, Oliver Jacob Hyams 1981-2018

Molly Rott & Leslie
In loving memory of Neal Rott, husband, father, son, and brother. Forever in our hearts.

Laura Summers
To my incredible parents, Julian and Anne Ruibal and my beloved son, Eric. You live forever in my heart."

Lolita Taylor
In loving memory of my Grama Betty Ann Davis

Jason Webdroff-Rawnicki
In loving memory of my little sister, Lauren – Thank you so much for the inspiration you give me each and every day. You are always with me. You will forever be my Doodie Ball.

Lisa Wilson
In loving memory of my beautiful son, Jahvon. As long as I live, you will never be forgotten. You will always be my Ace Boon Coon.

Camille Woods

To my son - Marcus, his best friend Big Jon and all the beautiful young people that leave this earth too soon. You are the lights we will look for when we come to join you.

# DISCLAIMER★★

This book contains the opinions and ideas of its authors. It is intended to provide helpful and informative material on the subjects addressed. However, it is written with the understanding that the authors and publisher are not engaged in rendering medical, mental health, or any other type of personal professional services. The ideas expressed in this book are not to be taken as endorsements or recommendations for the reader to follow as solutions to their health concerns.

The reader is strongly encouraged to consult with their healthcare team, including medical and mental health professionals, before adopting any suggestions from this book or drawing inferences from its content. The authors and publisher are sharing personal experiences and methods that have worked for them individually. They expressly disclaim any responsibility for any liability, loss, or risk—personal or otherwise—that may be incurred as a consequence, directly or indirectly, of the use and application of any content within this book. This includes, but is not limited to, the cessation of any personalized treatment without prior consultation with a professional healthcare team.

# INTRO

As a Psychologist, I've worked with at risk populations for over 26 years. Overdose. Suicide. Abuse. The list goes on.

And all of my education and experience meant absolutely nothing when I unexpectedly lost my husband, Jim:

my best friend, my soulmate.

And all that the hospital gave me was a hug. Not a resource. Not a phone number. Not a business card. Not even a pamphlet.

Thankfully, because of my background, I knew who to call and what to do to get immediate professional support. The average person doesn't.

And it infuriated me.

As time passed and people got back to their own busy lives, I learned how much support I truly needed - and couldn't find! Anywhere.

I was overwhelmed every time a task came, such as closing an account or presenting Jim's death certificate. And I wanted help. I looked for help.

And I was blown away by how little support is actually available.

The fire inside me grew.

I vowed to create the services that I couldn't find so others don't have to experience what I did. Griefhab is literally rehab for grief. Because there's rehab for everything else.

And because those dealing with loss are often looked at as if we're aliens. People shy away from the awkward and uncomfortable. So the burden lies on *us*.

Those *already* struggling.

Fueling my fire!

I went out into the world looking to break stigmas and provide support, and what I inadvertently discovered is that even other professionals are unaware.

Just like I was! Until I lost Jim.

Grief is the one thing we will all experience. More than once. It *does not* discriminate.

So why can't we all come together?

*Faces of Grief* is a step in that direction. What began as a book to help people struggling through loss and to help their loved ones has turned into a movement.

A movement to break stigmas and to change laws. A movement to *have the uncomfortable conversations* instead of avoiding them. A movement towards change.

Not next month or next year.

Today!

It's important for you to know that *whatever* loss you're going through, you matter. You're not alone. And it's my sincere hope that this book will help you understand that you *will* get through it - even if you can't see how today.

You'll get through it *your way.* And at your own pace!

Healing involves tuning out all the noise. People mean well, but only you know your path forward!

Even if you think you don't.

Let this book be your guide. Let the communities and resources shared be your lifelines in the tumultuous waters.

And let yourself accept the support.

While no two losses are identical, finding people who understand is part of the path towards healing. You don't have to let go of your friends and family. But please consider letting someone who gets it in!

Because Healing Happens Together ♥

# table of contents

*table of contents*

*Faces of grief*

*table of contents*

# CHOOSING JOY

By Alexa Bigwarfe

Hearing "Choose joy" may feel like an offensive statement if you're early in your grieving process. So let's get clear on what I mean. The purpose of this essay is not to tell you to get over it, as you may have heard from others. And it's not to tell you to leave your grief behind and move on. Instead, I want to provide some tools that may help you move forward when you're ready to begin your healing process.

One question that many people have is how much time does it take to get over a significant loss?

It's been my experience that we never get over losing the people we love the most. But that doesn't mean we can't find joy, peace, and even happiness when the time is right.

But sometimes, we must choose to get on this path, even if we don't want to. We don't choose for these terrible things to happen to us, but we do get to choose how we respond to them. We can remain bitter and sad for an endless number of days, stuck in our grief, or we can allow ourselves to heal. We can make the choice to find joy again.

If the idea of choosing joy right now makes you want to punch me in the face, then you're probably still in the heavy grief period and you may need to come back to this later. However, I want you to consider that joy and pain can, and often, co-exist. You can still be sad and also make the choice to open your heart to happiness again.

My infant daughter died in my arms when she was two days old. In those early days, I never could have imagined feeling whole and happy again. I believed that no matter what happened in my life, I would always have a Kathryn-sized hole that would keep me from being happy. But I can tell you that with time—processing each minute, each hour, each day… focusing on just surviving those moments—eventually, I found my heart was healing, piece by piece. But I also had to allow that process to happen.

It's okay to be sad. It's okay to grieve. And it's okay to experience joy alongside those feelings. It's been years since my daughter died, and I still have days that I'm overcome with sadness. I still cry occasionally. I mourn the life that I never got to live with her. That's a part of the grieving process, and it may follow us our entire lives. But it's also okay to take action steps that help you heal.

So if you are ready and willing to take the steps to move through or continue your healing process after your loss, then keep reading. Congratulations on making a conscious effort to choose joy rather than sadness. Or at least trying to get on that path.

Know and understand that this is a process that happens over time. Healing happens on *your* timeline, not on anyone else's. There may be setbacks and hard days, but the most important step is the one you take to heal *today*.

## Finding Joy After Loss

So many of us worry if we allow happiness back into our hearts, it means we are moving on and we are forgetting our loved ones. I promise you—you CAN allow joy back into your heart, you can find happiness again, AND you can remember and love your person.

### Step One: Ask for Help

We all need the time to grieve appropriately. When I'm talking with mothers who have lost their children, I often remind them to give themselves grace. The average heavy grieving period for a significant loss is eighteen to twenty-four months. So don't beat yourself up if it's only been a few months and you're still struggling. At this point, you should be. But when you start to reach the eighteen-month mark, if life isn't getting better—and definitely if you cross the two-year point without feeling like you're able to move on—it may be time to seek professional help.

Choosing to get help when you're grieving is a big step to healing. I knew that I needed extra help to survive the death of my daughter Kathryn. I asked for medication and began a low dose of Sertraline, which is the generic version of Zoloft. My doctor increased my dose after a few months, and I stayed on the medication for almost five years. Eventually I realized I was ready to live life without that assistance. Some people never get there, and that's okay too. That's between you and your doctor.

I also sought help from a therapist. I cannot tell you how helpful it was to visit a stranger and share all the feelings that I didn't feel I could share with anyone else. There are so many programs that help you process trauma. Thankfully, as a wider emphasis is placed on mental health, new initiatives are becoming available. And trying unconventional therapies, such as EFT (emotional freedom tapping) and equine therapy, has allowed me to connect with myself and to nature and heal in a beautiful way.

Step Two: Incorporate Self-Care and Healing Activities into Your Routine

This can be very challenging in the beginning. We often overlook the importance of caring for ourselves when we are grieving. It's hard enough to make it through each day, but then add on the responsibilities of caring for other children or a spouse or partner, or working a busy job, and who has the time and energy to focus on caring for themselves? And yet, if you want to heal, you're going to have to put yourself first, even if only for a few minutes each day.

There will be many days that you will be tempted to say, "I'll do it tomorrow." But you can't put it off. Start with small things. Maybe go on a short walk. Maybe write for three minutes in your journal.

Maybe just take a longer than usual shower or bath. But conscious efforts to take care of yourself can go a long way.

These are some of the activities that helped me focus and ground myself during my healing journey:

- Making the choice to change my thoughts and feelings.
- Journaling and writing.
- Serving others—I found ways to give back and helping other people who were experiencing a similar loss helped me.
- Finding ways to keep her memory alive every day.
- Laughing as often as possible.
- Spending time doing things that make me feel better. Water is one of those outlets, and I go to the water as often as I can.
- Surrounding myself with people who lifted me up, and made me feel seen and heard.
- Crying and grieving when I needed to do so.
- Making the time to breathe.
- Practicing gratitude.
- Finding ways to ground myself.
- Getaways with friends and loved ones.

There is also a lot of research-based evidence on the four key components that can help a person heal: practicing breathwork, doing gratitude practices, focusing on relationships and community, and making time for self-care.

It may take some experimentation to see which methods will work best for you, but the important thing is that you take action and do something.

Step Three: Find Community
Spend time with the people who love and care about you, and if you don't have anyone in your life that fits that description, look for grief

support groups or communities, like Griefhab, that will bring you in contact with people who understand what you're going through.

Community has been a tremendous part of my healing. In the months after my daughter died, I found Facebook groups with other mothers who walked a similar path. I found other people who knew and understood the pain of significant loss. And they provided an outlet for me that most people in my life could not. The grieving mother community has been a tremendous source of strength for me because they truly understand what I have been through, they validate my feelings, and we all share similar stories.

Whoever your inner circle is, find those people and make time to connect. Your spouse, best friend, siblings, neighbor, new friends—whoever they may be. A Harvard Study of Adult Development, which spanned seventy-five years, examined what makes people the happiest. The results were clear. The answer is in community and deep relationships. Close-knit relationships provide shelter against loneliness and sadness.

Losing a loved one can be a significantly isolating event. It might be easiest for you to turn away from the people who love you the most, but I encourage you to let them in. Or if you can't, find a new community that understands you.

**Begin your healing when you are ready and on your terms**

Probably the most important lesson I have learned in the past twelve years is that no one's grief journey is the same as another's. We may share similar feelings and experiences, but some of us heal quickly while others may take years to find a place of peace. And sadly, others will never get there.

The truth is, I don't know what will help YOU specifically.

I know that for me, the ultimate path to healing is to *choose joy*. You have to make the CHOICE to get there. Understand and know you will have setbacks. But pick yourself up and keep trying.

Every day I make the choice to take care of myself and to love myself. Some days I'm more successful than others. But I'm still moving forward. Most importantly, I am living my life to honor my daughter's short one. I am present in this life. I make a conscious decision each day to move forward and to seek healing.

It is my wish that you will find healing, joy, and happiness as well. And always remember, you are not alone.

If you've lost a child, a resource you might look into is *Sunshine After the Storm: A Survival Guide for the Grieving Mother*, which is an excellent resource for those who support grieving parents, those who want to understand grieving parents, and those who are grieving. The back of the book contains a full resource list of additional tools to help. Another resource is *Sisterhood of the Healing Hearts: Permission to Thrive. A Six-Month Guided Journal for Grieving Mothers*, a guided journal to help you implement daily healing activities. Both of these resources can be found on the website: https://sunshineafterthestorm.org

Alexa Bigwarfe is a USA Today Best-Selling author, speaker, and publishing consultant. Alexa turned to writing books as a healing method after the death of her infant daughter and fell in love with all things publishing. Her first book, *Sunshine After the Storm: A Survival Guide for the Grieving Mother*, led to the creation of a nonprofit, Sunshine After the Storm, to support grieving mothers. She is also the creator behind the healing journal *Sisterhood of the Healing Hearts: Permission to Thrive. A Six-Month Guided Journal for Grieving Mothers*. Alexa often works with writers who want to use writing as a healing tool, since writing was such an important piece of her healing journey. If you're interested in resources for Writing to Heal, grab them here: https://writepublishsell.com/writing-grief-free-5-day-challenge/

# BELOW THE SURFACE: EXPLORING ADOPTION'S DEEP-SEATED GRIEF

*By Elizabeth Barbour*

I arrived in this world, in this body, at 1:52 a.m. on a cold, blustery winter day in January in upstate New York. When my mother delivered me, there was no fanfare, no balloons, no celebration. There was no husband, no mother, no sister to coach her through labor. There were no kind words, no empathy, no grief counseling. She was all alone in a sterile hospital ward filled with fluorescent lights and doctors and nurses rushing to and fro, who paid little mind to her. When it came time for my entrance, they administered sleeping gas to her and she was knocked unconscious.

Did I arrive quietly and quickly? Or did I resist the inevitable and howl the entire way? I'll never know. All I know is that I was a whopping 8 lbs. 11 ozs. according to my birth certificate. The nursing team whisked me away to the nursery. I never smelled my mother, never touched her, never saw her.

Imagine a baby in the womb. It's dark and cramped but cozy and secure. There are certain sounds and familiar smells associated with that incubator. Then, when the child is born, they travel through the birth canal into the light. They become aliens in a strange land.

Bright lights, strange smells, jarring sounds. It's an assault to the senses. But most babies get placed on their mother's belly, and her touch, her smell, and her familiar rhythmic voice offer comfort to ease the transition.

I didn't have that bonding time. Neither did my mother.

⌀

Kathy woke up after the sleeping gas wore off and looked around to realize she was all alone. In her groggy state, she searched for me and became very confused. She began to panic. *Where is my baby?*

Still confused and disoriented, she strained to climb out of bed and shuffled to the door. She took a few steps down the hallway and two orderlies noticed her. They stepped in front of her to block her path.

"My baby. Where's my baby? I want to see my baby," she demanded. "Where's the nursery?"

They shook their heads, ignoring her pleas.

"We must take you back to your room."

Two orderlies, one on each side of her, held her arms securely with their hands and steered her back to her room.

"But I want to see my baby!"

⌀

In the 1960s and 1970s, unwed mothers were treated with disdain, disrespect, and disgust. Any woman who "got herself in that predicament" was surely unsavory, and not a "good girl" or from a "good family." She was a second-class citizen, often sent away to have her baby in secret at an unwed mother's home or shipped off (as my mother was) to a relative living in another town in hopes of preserving her reputation when she returned home.

But going home was excruciating. No one (except her own mother, the person who sent her away to try and hide the shame from the family's reputation) knew of Kathy's pregnancy, of her pain, of her loss. No one knew about the nights she cried herself to sleep, about how her milk came in and she didn't know how to stop it. How she thought about her baby all the time. *What does she look like? Does she have all ten fingers and toes? Does she have hair? Does she look like me or her father?*

That's where the real pain was.

He'd said *no*. He said, "I can't, I won't."

He said, "I'm not sure it's even my kid."

Yet he filled out the paperwork that the adoption agency sent to him. She gave them his name, but she didn't put it on my birth certificate. It's as though she wanted to claim me for herself. She didn't want to share me with him.

But she never even got to see me.

Meet Joan. Considered an old maid in 1970 at the age of thirty-six, her heart had longed for a decade for a child to love. But because of her medical history—starting with her first surgery at age thirteen for ovarian cysts and ending with her fifth surgery, a radical hysterectomy, almost two decades later—she thought her dreams of having a family were doomed. The grief was thick, and her longing was like a bottomless pit.

She signed up with the local adoption agency, not knowing what to expect. She kept herself busy with her work as a secretary and her heart's work of raising and showing champion poodles. Her star female, Beaujolais, had a litter of eight, who she diligently and discriminately found perfect homes for.

So, when the agency called to say, "We have a baby for you!" she was elated. The social worker arrived at the front doorstep with a tiny two-week-old baby, her jet-black hair sticking straight up and an angry red rash covering her body from head to toe. "We know she's ugly," she said. "You don't have to keep her."

Joan snatched that baby from the arms of that social worker and claimed the child as her own. I became hers in a millisecond.

~~~~~~~

I grew up surrounded by love. My parents adored me, doted on me. So much so that they smothered me. Later in life, Joan proudly and somewhat sheepishly confessed, "I was a helicopter parent long before it was 'a thing.' I just wanted to keep you safe from harm."

Despite their love and devotion, I never felt like I belonged. I didn't look like them. Or act like them. Or think like them. My mom always said, "I just don't understand you, child!" which alienated me even further.

Even though my parents talked openly about my adoption, we never acknowledged the trauma involved. Every year on my birthday, Mom would say "There's a young woman out there in the world thinking about you today." For a moment, that would bring me a glimmer of hope and then, privately, I'd fixate on the fact that she wasn't in my life *now*.

It wasn't until I started therapy in college that I started to understand why I felt like a stranger in a strange land. It's because I was. I was drowning in grief, unconscious of its presence in the foundation of my life.

After searching for three-and-a-half years, I finally met my biological family for the first time at age twenty-nine and reunited with my birth mother, my birth father, and eleven (!) siblings. My initial meeting with Kathy was one of the most profound experiences of my life. Roger, my birth father, also welcomed me with open arms. The early years of our reunion were filled with joy and laughter and curiosity and long conversations, trying to learn my family history and build relationships with my new blood relatives.

But it also stirred up a lot of pain, confusion, and uncertainty. I continuously questioned my identity, trying to navigate the complex tapestry of having an adoptive family and a biological family. Who was I now that I had a more complete foundation?

In my mid-thirties, as I was wrestling with some post-reunion issues with my adoptive mother and birthmother, I worked with a therapist who specialized in family constellations work. I was torn by my extreme loyalty to Joan, yet my undeniable connection to Kathy.

The facilitator looked me squarely in the face and proclaimed, "Elizabeth, you have four parents."

At first, I gazed at him quizzically, not comprehending.

"You have your adoptive mom and adoptive dad who raised you. And you have your biological mom and biological dad who created you. You have four parents," he stated.

It was the first time someone had spoken the truth to me. As I let that new reality settle into my bones, I felt a sense of clarity and peace wash over me. It was as though I had been wearing fogged up glasses and someone wiped them off and I was seeing everything in focus for the first time.

From there on, I learned how to carry the both/and. I could be grateful for the incredible gifts my parents raised me with—an abundance of love, a commitment to education, an appreciation for classical music, a desire to travel, a hunger for winning at Scrabble. And I could simultaneously grieve what I'd lost—growing up with my biological parents, missing out on having siblings growing up, feeling comfortable in my body, feeling connected and bonded by blood and shared DNA.

During my adoption reunion, Joan also learned to carry the both/ and. She had grieved her infertility long ago, but when I discovered my birth family, she faced her fear of losing me to my biological family. The grief that she now had to "share me" was hard to swallow. She bravely supported my decision to search and reunite and as the years went on, she realized that she hasn't lost a daughter, but that I simply gained another mother (but not another Mom) and more family. In fact, our relationship improved over time because my knowledge of my ancestry helped me to be more solid and confident in my sense of self and identity.

I often describe meeting Kathy as though I found answers to questions I didn't know that I had. She, too, learned to carry the both/and. For three decades, she'd carried around a canyon of grief and shame for her decision to place me for adoption, and wished she'd had been strong enough to fight her mother, who had forced her to give me up. But I assured her that I trusted the Divine Will orchestrating all of this and knew that Joan and Ron were supposed to be my parents, and what was she supposed to do in the 1970s anyway? Society was not kind to unwed mothers back then and our lives—both hers and mine—would likely have been compromised in different ways had she raised me.

The current system of adoption is complex at best. Built on grief and loss, all triad members—birth parents, adoptive parents and adoptees—are likely to suffer enormous trauma. Children are separated from their biological family at birth. First mothers (and sometimes fathers) make the impossible decision to choose an adoption plan for their child because they are unable to parent or don't feel supported in doing so. Adoptive parents often (not always) grieve their own infertility, which may include miscarriages and infant loss before they seek adoption as a pathway to building a family.

Fortunately, modern adoption practices encourage openness. Research studies have shown that honesty, transparency, and connection benefit all members of the adoption triad when it's possible to have healthy relationships. But it's not always possible.

Healing progress can be made for all triad members with the aid of therapy, coaching, support groups, and reading adoption literature. Reunions that are positive and constructive can be life-changing and life-giving for all parties involved. Navigating the reunion with intention and guidance is critical because a myriad of emotions—grief, sorrow, anger, joy, celebration, hope—are all part of the mix. Reunions that don't go well can exacerbate wounds that already exist and cause even more pain, confusion, and loss.

Every family impacted by adoption has a different experience. I've been incredibly fortunate to have had a fairytale reunion for twenty-five years. We've worked hard to make memories together and despite geographical distance, I've attended as many graduations, weddings, and birthdays as possible (with eleven siblings, that's a lot!). After knowing them for all this time, I've had a chance to work through much of my pain and loss.

I've met plenty of people with stories like mine, and there are just as many tales of heartache. Challenging reunions or no reunions at all are just as common. I know triad members who initially reunited with relatives, but the connection fizzled out quickly. I know several adoptees who found their ancestral lineage, only to discover their parents were deceased. I've met adoptees who were afraid to search for fear of upsetting their adoptive parents, and I've met biological parents who avoid searching because of the shame they feel about creating an adoption plan for their child. I also know adoptive parents who struggle to truly bond with their children, whether they were adopted as infants or as older children.

The trauma of not knowing our roots, losing connection with a loved one, or feeling concern for the safety and well-being of your child are all byproducts of the challenging system of adoption.

But the truth is, being human is hard. Whether you're impacted by adoption or not, the chances are good that you've felt like an outsider or like you didn't fit at some point in your life. Struggling with our identity is part of our growth and experience on this planet. As Richard Bach says in his spiritual classic *Illusions*, "The bond that links your true family is not one of blood, but of respect and joy in each other's life. Rarely do members of the same family grow up under the same roof." The good news is that with friends, neighbors, coworkers, and family, too, you can create your own circle of belonging.

Since 2000, Elizabeth Barbour has coached women through life's challenges, drawing from her own experiences that include divorce, parental loss, adoption-related struggles, infertility, health issues, and relocations. Through her Solid Ground program, Elizabeth models how grief and gratitude can live side by side, teaching the power of self-care and rituals. An intuitive coach and shamanic practitioner, she blends traditional techniques with ancient wisdom.

Elizabeth, a reunited adoptee and adoptive mother, found her birth mother, birth father and eleven brothers and sisters in 1999, and has developed meaningful relationships with all in the past twenty-five years. Her daughter, Riley, was adopted in a semi-open adoption and they've been living in a joyful reunion with her biological father for four years. Whether coaching, speaking or leading retreats, she continues to attract adoptees, adoptive parents, and birth parents into her sphere.

Elizabeth is also the author of the award-winning *Sacred Celebrations: Designing Rituals to Navigate Life's Milestone Transitions* and *Smart Self-Care for Busy Women: 20 Lessons to Help You Create the "Me Time" You Keep Putting Off.*

She lives in the magical mountains of Asheville, North Carolina, with her family and soul friends.

Join her Facebook group
www.facebook.com/groups/sacredcelebrations
Follow her on Instagram
www.instagram.com/elizabthbarbour
Set up a free introductory fifteen-min call at
www.elizabethbarbour.com/coaching.

# BRIDGES: FROM DESPAIR, TO ACCEPTANCE, TO RESILIENCE

*By James S. Bergquist*

*I want to preface this chapter by stating that, due to the nature of my story, the original names and places involved have been changed.*

## DESPAIR

My son died on a Friday afternoon on a cold, snowy day in Connecticut. At the time, he was healthy and strong. He was a decent, hardworking young man with a bright future. But on that fateful afternoon, my son was convicted of a crime he did not commit. He was found guilty of sexually assaulting a child—his own six-year-old daughter. He did not die in the literal, physical sense, but on that day, it felt like his life was over.

My son, David, and his ex-girlfriend, Mary, met in Boston. Their relationship was fraught with raging arguments and hostility. They never married, but they did have a daughter together. Suddenly and without warning, Mary returned to Connecticut, taking their daughter with her. My son stayed in Boston and continued to work on a commercial fishing boat.

After several years apart, David decided to leave fishing and move to Connecticut. He missed his daughter immensely and the separation was hard to endure. He wanted to be the father he knew he could be, the father he wanted to be, the father his little girl needed.

He and Mary rented a small apartment. They wanted to make the relationship work for the sake of their daughter—a fresh start. David worked full-time at a local convenience store.

My son thought he had found paradise. He was working, helping to support his family, and he truly enjoyed being a father to his daughter. Despite his tumultuous relationship with Mary, he was happy. He missed fishing, but that was a price he was willing to pay.

As time went on, his relationship with Mary began to deteriorate again. There were more arguments and fights, more yelling and screaming, and more police visits to their small apartment.

David and Mary decided to start seeing a counselor. During one of their counseling sessions, Mary confided that when their daughter was a toddler, she had touched her inappropriately.

My son was livid. During their subsequent arguments, he would bring up Mary's molestation of their daughter. "I am going to the police. I am going to get custody of her. You are a child molester! Do you hear me? I am going to report you to the police! I am going to get our daughter and you will be in jail!"

My son held those threats over Mary's head like a wrecking ball. She begged my son not to report her to the police. She was consumed with fear that she would lose their daughter and that she would indeed go to jail.

My son never notified the police. However, Mary took the threats seriously, very seriously.

After one horrific argument, my son once again threatened to have Mary arrested and then abruptly left their apartment. Afraid that she would go to jail and lose her daughter, Mary called the police and made up a story that my son had sexually assaulted their daughter. My son was arrested.

Immediately after his arrest, his daughter underwent a thorough medical exam. The exam failed to reveal any sexual assault or sexual contact of any kind.

His daughter was also interviewed extensively by the lead detective on the case. After the interview, the detective sent an email to the prosecutor. In the email, the detective stated, "It appears that the child has been coached." But during the trial, the judge ruled that the email reflected the detective's "opinion" and it was not admissible as evidence.

So, despite the absence of physical or forensic evidence of a crime, and the lack of any corroborating witnesses, my son was convicted.

When the verdict was read, my son's knees buckled. His eyes began to twitch wildly, darting from the police officer standing next to him, to the attorney, to me. His mouth opened, and his face flushed. He was in a daze.

He was sentenced to thirty years in prison, and we found ourselves in the midst of a hellish new world.

## ACCEPTANCE

Every day I am haunted by the anguish that my son is in the deep, dark hole that is prison. Prison is about fear, intimidation, and control. Reduced to its simplest terms, every hour is a battle to survive. My son went from being a respected crew member of a commercial fishing vessel on the open sea to being stripped of his dignity and confined to an eight-by-ten-foot cell.

Mentally, I refused to accept what had happened. I could not bring myself to say "prison," "cell," or "inmate." I would say "facility," "room" and "roommate instead" Using euphemisms allowed me to deny the harsh reality that my son was in prison.

Reluctantly, I came to realize that sugar-coating our situation did not benefit either of us.

For the past seven years, I have worked toward accepting my son's fate—our fate. So, what could we do? In my eyes, acceptance is different from giving up or losing hope. It means coming to grips with reality. It means figuring out how to exist, to find a path forward, to make a plan.

Yesterday is gone. We do not get it back.

I try not to dwell on all the normal moments and events my son has missed, all the birthdays, holidays, and anniversaries. I try not to think about the last time we played catch, or went to a movie, or to the mall to buy something as mundane as a pair of socks. I was able to find inner peace knowing that my son was accepting of the situation because of his belief in God and the comfort and reassurance knowing that it would all work out... that this had happened to him for a reason, that he was in prison for a reason... only known to God.

Instead, I formulated a plan. Every day I find one thing to be thankful for. I stay positive. To me, acceptance is an attitude that is developed over time. Someone once said, "aAction is an antidote for despair."

Breaking it down further, I have devised a way for my plan to work. I have what I call the "word of the week." Examples of these words include faith, belief, hope, acceptance, trust, future, thankful, strength, patience, control, perspective, and surrender.

What does this accomplish? These words keep me focused on staying positive, on looking forward and not dwelling on the past. I am not trying to move a mountain. I am just trying to move.

When my son was convicted and sent to prison, I began a brutal wrestling match with God and the incomprehensible injustice of my son being wrongfully convicted. I was at a crossroads: I could either keep fighting or I could accept the reality of it all. I could either work against God or I could work through Him.

My son had been taken away from me and it hurt. I realized that I could not fix it myself. I could not make it better myself. I could not change it myself. My healing started with just one simple word: help. I prayed that God would help my son and me find a positive way forward.

I was able to find peace. Believing in God's plan has helped me navigate the sadness, depression, and frustration that I feel, and helps me keep hope alive. And I truly believe in God's plan for both of us. I visualize my son's freedom and I trust the Lord to get us through our challenges.

I usually walk out to our pasture around sunset to feed our horses. It is completely quiet except for a few birds chirping in the trees. There, in the solitude and silence of the moment, under a sunset that only God can create, I pray. If I am wearing a hat, I take it off and look up at the sunset and the sky. I ask the Lord to watch over my son and protect him. "Dear Lord, please help us accept our situation and help us get through tomorrow."

Alone in the pasture, no one can see me shed tears for my son.

## RESILIENCE

I think about, dream about, and believe in my son's future, when he is free, when he is home. When he can lead a normal life, have a good job, meet someone, have a family. When he can be with family and friends.

There is a small sign in my barn that reads, "With God, all things are possible." I have repeated that phrase one thousand times and continually pray that God will find a way to set my son free.

Recently, during a church service, the congregation sang a praise song. There was a verse in the song that went "…and He will set the prisoner free."

When I heard that, it was like being struck by a bolt of lightning. That verse has stuck with me. I repeat it over and over.

Soon after that day, David called me. He said he had been watching Dr. David Jeremiah, a Christian author and founder of Turning Point Radio and Television Ministries, and had started reading several Christian books about the Bible and "God's plan." He said there are good days and bad days, but you cannot cherry pick which days you want to trust in the Lord.

After that, it seemed as though my son's whole attitude had suddenly changed. He was at peace. He told me that listening to Dr. Jeremiah's programs inspired him to get out of his cell bunk every day. He said, "Dad, how can those passages from the Bible not be messages from God?" He said he listens to Dr. Jeremiah's words and thinks about how they relate to his past, his present, and his future.

And then it hit me. My son *is* free. His spirit, his soul, his mind, his heart are free. God had answered my prayers, but in His own way, not in the way that I had prayed for.

Context matters.

We stay positive. He gets cards and letters and personal visits from my wife and I, and we talk on the phone almost daily. I put money in his commissary account so he can order whatever he needs. My son practices yoga, exercises, writes, and reads. He never fails to make me laugh when we talk on the phone. Sometimes when he calls, he will reminisce about his time on the fishing boat. It's one fishing story after another. During that half-hour call, I might get two words in!

I still pray that one day, hopefully soon, my son and I will be able to sit together on our porch, share a cup of coffee, and watch our horses graze peacefully under a vibrant North Carolina sunset.

It comes down to time. My son is in prison. Doing time. If I could only have more time with my son, more free time. Generally, people think they have all the time in the world. Plenty of time. Time to plan. Time to dream. Time to spare. Time for another cup of coffee. Time to read another good book. Time to watch another brilliant sunset. Time to pick up a baseball and play catch. Time to hold hands and tell someone *I love you.* All the time in the world to take the precious moments that make life so special for granted. Then, like a swift, punishing, unexpected punch to the gut, we realize that all the time in the world is still not enough.

If there is one thing I would like to share by writing this story, it is this: It is easy to take for granted someone you see every day, whether it is your spouse, your children, your mother, or your father.

Appreciate the time you spend with them. Embrace the moments that you share.

It has been quite a journey. My son and I have crossed many bridges over troubled water. How, when, and where our journey ends are answers only known to God.

My first novel, *Beyond the Rainbow*, was released in 2022 and was inspired by the true events that occurred in my son's case. The life of the main character is an arc, connecting his past life as a fisherman and a father to his present life as a prison inmate. Writing the book was cathartic and helped me process the misery and frustration that I was experiencing.

I wrote "Bridges" to help others who are coping with their own feelings of grief. In my own case, I had to come to grips with the fact that my son had been taken away. We both needed a path forward to get through each and every day. Our journey is based on acceptance, support, and hope. It took time, but with God's help, we did it.

The novel is fiction based on real events, but this chapter is about me, a real person, and my experiences. My story is also an arc, starting with the early despair I felt at my son's conviction and ending with how I learned to accept his situation and move forward with hope and faith.

**James S. Bergquist** is a screenwriter and freelance writer who grew up in Southern California. He holds a Bachelor of Science degree in political science and history as well as a Juris Doctorate degree. He lives with his wife in North Carolina. For more information, comments, or inquiries, please visit www. itsacreativeidea.com.

# UNCONDITIONAL LOVE

By Kristina Bottenberg

I am no stranger to trauma.

I was born into it and learned over the years that these two things, trauma and grief, can be interrelated and grief can come in many degrees and forms. From the earliest time I can remember, I was sexually molested by the hands of my father.

I guess this was really my first encounter with grief. I grieved (and still do) for a father and a childhood I did not have and can never possibly have. This set me up to have emotional problems and make poor decisions as I grew up. I had absolutely no self-worth, self-esteem, or confidence. In fact I hated myself, and was depressed and miserable.

As a teen, I got pregnant by my first real boyfriend. It was a terribly abusive relationship, and he attempted to end my life by forcibly playing Russian roulette with me. When I learned I was pregnant. I mustered the courage to leave because I knew I wanted this baby and needed to keep it safe. Even back then, when I was a young mother who didn't know what I was doing, I knew I had to keep my baby safe. Even though I ached for this relationship with this man, to this day I know I just wanted to be loved. But to me, that meant I deserved to be hurt. Once my baby girl, Kenzie, was born, she became my everything and I finally knew unconditional love.

However, I continued to make poor choices and ended up in physically, emotionally, and verbally abusive relationships. One after another.

But during these trials, there were good times as well. I had two more daughters who are also my world. Even though I was struggling as a single mother, we loved each other, and I tried to do special things with them. But I was still struggling with severe depression and PTSD from my childhood and relationships. I was angry at life and the hand I'd been dealt.

Then, I lost my brother. We had grown up together, and I'd gotten very close to him later in life. At thirty-six, he was diagnosed with cancer and given six months to live. He fought for thirteen. He was so brave, and I was so very proud of him, but also scared. When he passed, it was my first real experience with the death of someone close to me. I had lost grandparents and was sad when that happened. But they had lived far away and I rarely saw them, so their deaths did not hit close.

Then, everything changed. I worked most often as a bartender, and one day a man walked into my place of employment who taught me what it felt like to be loved. I had never been with someone who loved me unconditionally and completely. He quickly became my husband and a wonderful father to my girls. He was especially close to my youngest daughter, and she to him. There was no question who her father was—she adored him 100 percent.

Life was finally good. There was work, school, sports, vacations, camping, and fishing. We loved doing these things and spending time with each other. I was content, loved, and happy. I'd had such a hard life and been through so much, and I was finally catching a break with the man I loved and my wonderful daughters and two bonus daughters. Everything I'd been through seemed just a bit more tolerable now that I had this man in our lives.

But my life was about to change, and I was about to experience grief, trauma, and hardship like nothing else. Everything I had been through before paled in comparison. To this day, if I had not been living it, I wouldn't have believed it. I believe my mind often still doesn't fully comprehend what happened—maybe as a coping mechanism.

Let's back up to the beginning of 2021 when the COVID-19 pandemic was in full force. My oldest daughter, Kenzie, had announced a pregnancy, and was about five and a half months along. She already had a ten-year-old daughter who is an absolute joy to me. I call her my super baby. Kenzie had waited a long time to try for another and hadn't been sure she would be able to have more children. Everyone was so excited, trying to guess whether it would be a boy or girl. For my part, I was having another grandchild and could not wait. My mom, daughters, granddaughter, and I are all very close, so we thought what better than a girl's night to celebrate having the baby.

By this time, businesses were up and running, although masks were still required. So, we booked a hotel room at a local casino that had family friendly activities such as bowling. Perfect, let bowl! Kenzie started feeling poorly, so she chose to sit out and just watch us, but she was still happy and in good spirits. After bowling we headed back to the room to continue girls' night. By this time, Kenzie was feeling chilled and a lot worse. We stayed through the night, and the next day Kenzie was still feeling poorly but didn't have a fever. We all said our goodbyes and went home.

What I'm now about to tell you is to the best of my recollection because everything from there is a blur, very traumatic, and very painful. I went to work the next day as it was a Monday, and my daughter called me from the ER stating she had covid and was coughing up blood. She would be staying the night.

I was worried about her and the baby, but honestly not overly concerned. She was only twenty-eight and I really hadn't heard of covid killing young people. My uncle had been in critical condition and survived it, and he was much older. Death was far from my thoughts.

We got the call a week later, sometime before midnight, saying we needed to come now. We did not make it. My daughter was gone. I would never hear her voice again. Never laugh with her again or get a hug along with so much more that I and the rest of her family will forever miss out on. I saw what no parent should ever see—their child lying there with no life left in their body.

I was and still am heartbroken. I had no clue what to do next. I thought what now? I had lost my first-born baby, the beautiful woman who had made me a mother, who had truly saved my life. She'd left a new son whom she would never meet or hold. She'd also left her daughter, a husband, many family members and friends and me, her mother, all of us lost, angry, with so many questions, and so much regret. Hating God.

I didn't and honestly still don't understand why I had to lose my daughter after all the trauma and grief and hardships I had already endured in life. I didn't know why God was punishing me, but that's exactly how I felt. I knew my life would be forever be changed,

I had always needed my husband, but after Kenzie passed, I needed him more than ever. I knew he would be my rock. He would stay by my side while I continued to battle the demons that were back, full force, in my head. All the questions, the what ifs, the should haves, the *Did I do enough? Did I show her enough love? Did she know I loved her? Had I been the mother she deserved?* I really beat myself up over this.

Yes, my husband was there by my side to try and reassure and comfort me. I had managed to make it back to work. It was hard, but it also helped to distract me from what my reality was. Then, it was Aug 2, 2021, about three short months after the loss of my daughter. I was getting ready for work. My husband wasn't feeling great, so I was asking him whether he would be going to work that day. As he tried to get out of bed, he fell and was unintelligible. I couldn't understand what he was asking me, so I called 911. Usually, he would have protested that had I presented that option. He did not, so I knew I had to call. I knew something bad was happening, but no idea what. What then took place is also still unreal to me. The paramedics arrived and shortly after they had to start CPR.

In my mind, he was still going to be fine. He had battled a prescription narcotic dependency because of his doctor, so I thought maybe he'd taken a little too much. But Narcan was administered and that did nothing to help. The paramedics told me I needed to get a ride and meet them at the hospital.

My husband died on August 3, first thing in the morning. I was again feeling shock, disbelief, devastation, and fear, among so many other emotions. I don't remember how much time I took off that time. My work was good to me. But it wasn't too long before I had to go back because now I was living on a single income with one daughter still at home. But I was not thriving. I worked and slept, barely mothering my daughter, and wasting away because I couldn't eat. I decided I needed more help, so work gave me more time off, and I visited a wellness center. It was good for me while I was there, but I still came home to the same reality.

Eventually, I found Griefhab and Sam Ruth through a friend who had lost her brother. No matter what, Sam is there for me and believes in me even when I don't believe in myself and I falter along the way.

I'm still angry. I don't believe that all things happen for a reason. I'm still young in my grief and no matter where you are at, it's not wrong. It's ok if you aren't ok. I take one step forward and three steps back on some days, and on other days I may take only three steps back. And there's a day here and there where I manage to take a step forward. For example, one day I was driving after leaving my counselor's office and going back over our conversation in my head. She had told me it wouldn't always be this painful. My first thought was that I deserve this much pain because Kenzie mattered. Then, plain as day, I could hear her tell me that experiencing some joy does not make her life any less meaningful on this earth. That me finding some happiness does not mean she didn't matter. She changed my life for the good, forever, and no one can take that from me. Our memories are special and will always be with me.

Unfortunately, I know that no matter what joy or happiness I experience in life, I will always feel sad. For reasons I don't understand, this has been my path. But my journey is not over. And deep down, I still have hope for the future.

I was born November of 1973, in Monterey California, moving just a few short months after my birth to Germany. Being that my father was in the army we lived on the base there. Being an Army brat, I was accustomed to moving often. We spent a few years there before moving back to the U.S and finally settling in Washington state. Growing up I endured a lot of dysfunction and trauma. I persevered and throughout my early adult years had 3 beautiful, accomplished girls, one is now my guardian angel, my brightest star in the sky. I am in fact a grieving mother. I met my second husband Dave in 2013 and in 2014 we were married and so in love. I am in fact a grieving widow. I have 2 beautiful grandchildren from my angel Kenzie, and many bonus grandchildren through my late husband. I work full time in Skagit county, I enjoy my work, I also enjoy my 3 cats, hiking, kayaking, fishing, camping with family and friends. I am also taking this time to evaluate what's important; you could lose those people that mean so much to you in the blink of an eye. And finally, I'm trying to learn to love myself, I am taking baby steps on this journey. Life can change in ways that are so devastating, but I know there must be still beauty in living, that's why I haven't given up though there are times I want to. Even though I always will live with the grief and loss, because that will never go away, I have hope it will coincide with joy.

Kristina Bottenberg

# SEARCHING FOR WARMTH

*Brooke Carlock*

"I think they're dead."

Those were the only words I could make out as my ex-husband David screamed and sobbed hysterically at the other end of the phone. And then, *click*. Nothing. Icy fingers crept down my spine, leaving me cold and breathless. With one hand on the dashboard in front of me to steady my shaking body and one clutching my cell phone, I frantically dialed back, over and over, until he picked up again.

"I'm sorry I hung up on you," David said in a rush, no longer screaming, but still audibly panicked. "I need you to come here right now. The kids have been in an accident." He told me where he was headed: an intersection right next to a popular local farmer's market halfway between his house and mine. I relayed the location to my second husband, who immediately turned our car around and headed in that direction. I heard sirens wailing on the other end of the phone. Then David hung up again.

I rocked back and forth in the passenger's seat, arms wrapped around myself as though attempting to keep my insides from spilling out onto the floor mat. "No... no... no... no... no," I murmured, drips of cold sweat trickling down my back and peppering my forehead.

My husband drove as fast as he could, offering platitudes from the driver's seat. "I'm sure they're fine," he said. "I'm sure it's not that bad." But I knew. Call it mother's intuition, or the fact that in twenty-three years of being married to David I had never, ever heard his voice sound so terrified— I knew that it *was* that bad.

Police cars had blocked the area off and we yelled, "We're the parents!" as we wove around a maze of orange cones and flares. It was only 6:30 p.m., but the winter sky was already completely dark except for ominous flashing and flickers of red lights from police cars, ambulances, and fire trucks. Our car hadn't even rolled to a complete stop before I opened the door and leapt out. Nothing registered as I scanned the scene. There were so many flashing lights, so many people. I saw my son Max's car with its side smashed in and pieces of metal littering the road around it. A white sheet was draped over the passenger's side window and windshield.

I started walking toward Max's car in a daze, but then I heard David yelling my name, and I zeroed in on his voice, following the sound to the other side of the street. I looked up at his crumpled, tear-soaked face and saw confirmation of what I already knew.

"Libby didn't make it," he whispered.

It's strange that now, years later, the most vivid sensation I remember from that night, the night I lost my beautiful ten-year-old daughter, is the cold. The instant I heard David's voice on the other end of the phone, every ounce of warmth drained out of my body, and I couldn't get it back. The cold was so intense that I felt numb from the inside out. I was in shock. As David and a police officer explained to me that our eighteen-year-old son Max had been revived on the scene and taken by ambulance to the hospital, their voices sounded distant, as if

I were listening from under an ice-covered pond. I vaguely comprehended the officer telling me that I couldn't see my daughter's body because she had taken the full impact of the truck that had hit them.

Hours later, the cold still hadn't released its grip as David told me the full story: Max had picked Libby up from dance and was driving both of them to David's house. The check engine light came on, and Max had called David asking what to do about it. David had told Max to pull over in the farmer's market parking lot, and told him that he'd meet them there to check out the car. While still on the phone, David heard Libby scream, and the phone had gone dead.

I shivered as I stood by my son's hospital bed and looked at his bloody face and clothes, morbidly wondering which stains were his, and which his sister's. Even when the test results came back and I learned that Max's head injury wouldn't result in permanent damage—his memory loss would only be temporary—even when I was engulfed in hugs from my other son Grayson and our other family members, I couldn't get warm.

I was no stranger to grief. I'd lost both my sister and sister-in-law before they turned thirty-five. Just four months prior to the accident, I'd lost my dad unexpectedly when he'd had a heart attack in his car on his way home from work. Then, two weeks later, on the day of my dad's funeral, my stepmom overdosed on pills and alcohol and died. And my mom had been diagnosed with pancreatic cancer the month before the accident (she died fourteen months after Libby). Life had already made me the butt of its cosmic joke, and the punchline was always a new flavor of grief.

But none of this had prepared me for the devastation I felt from the loss of my daughter. And how could it have? She was my world. My mini-me. My barnacle, always stuck to my side. With her death, my world changed in an instant. There would be no more giggly after-school conversations on the car ride home. No more dance competitions. No more snuggles while watching *Little House on the Prairie*. No more singing our favorite Billy Joel song before bed.

How does someone go on after experiencing so much loss? For me, the cold and shock melted into a state of hyperfocus, distraction, and denial. I wrote every word of Libby's obituary and funeral service, made a photo slideshow and a video compilation of her dancing, and wrote thank you cards to family and friends. I didn't eat, I didn't sleep, and the whole time I felt like she was going to walk back in the door. But when the service was over, the cards sent out, and the house went quiet, reality set in and I collapsed.

One day, while visiting the crash site to add some decorations to Libby's roadside memorial, I found myself staring at the massive trucks whizzing by. I walked down the embankment to stand on the side of the busy two-lane road, feeling the wind whip my hair as the trucks barreled past. I stood there for a few minutes, contemplating how easy it would be to walk out in front of one of them. To die right there, in the same place as my daughter, and not have to carry the seemingly unbearable pain that I'd been shouldering any longer.

As I considered my options, a truck blew its horn and jarred me out of my daze. I ran back up the embankment to my car, where I climbed in and sobbed hysterically, screaming, "I HATE YOU!" at every truck that passed by. When I finally made it home, I phoned a local psychiatric hospital, enrolled in their intensive mental health day program, and started taking antidepressant and anti-anxiety medications. The more I thawed from the shock of Libby's death, the more I wondered if I would ever find a way back from the emptiness that had taken over my life.

The most frustrating thing about grief is that the world keeps turning, even when you're drowning in sorrow. I had two sons, Max and his sixteen year-old brother Grayson, who were still alive and grieving their sister. Bills still need to be paid, meals still need to be put on the table, laundry still needs folding. I returned to my teaching job one month after the accident, and I spent many evenings and weekends serving as a caregiver for my mom, who had started her chemotherapy treatments. I drove Max back and forth to his doctor's appointments and sessions with a trauma therapist. I also met with police officers and learned that Max was at fault for the accident. In his hurry to get to the farmer's market and meet his dad, he'd run through the stop sign at the intersection. From the very beginning, I made it my mission to assure Max that I didn't blame him for Libby's death. He was a careful driver and a responsible person. What happened was a tragic accident, and could've happened to anyone. More than anything, I didn't want the weight of loss to destroy the life of another of my children. Despite feeling completely and utterly overwhelmed most days, I held myself together as best as I could. I got very good at putting on a "fake face" during the day. At night, I allowed myself to fall apart.

I am admittedly a nerd. I love history and reading and learning. So in any spare second I had, I read books and articles about grief and watched every video on recovery that I could find. I also started a blog to share my experiences and feelings, mostly because I had what felt like a million people asking me "How are you?" every day, and it was easier to direct them there than to have an honest conversation. Getting my emotions out, even on a computer screen, helped immensely, and it also seemed to help other grieving people who managed to find my website. Learning and writing about grief started a spark that I hoped would help me find my way out of the cold.

Within a few months, I started posting regularly on social media and recording videos for YouTube with updates on my grief journey. My first videos were terrible! Truly, truly terrible. I had no idea what I was doing. Even so, I started receiving emails and getting comments from others, thanking me for sharing my story and being so open and honest about my grief. I realized that there were few people out there who had been through hell and were willing to talk about it.

Hearing that my work helped other people gave me a new sense of purpose. It made me feel like Libby, who had spent her short life doing anything she could to make people's lives better, would be proud of me. Every comment I received offered a little bit of warmth to my soul, and opened my eyes to how many people in the world were suffering. I wanted to offer them a perspective on grief from someone who understood them—who had been in the trenches and felt the excruciating, life-altering pain of many different types of loss.

By the time the one-year anniversary of Libby's death rolled around, my entire life had changed. I divorced my second husband and become a single empty nester as both of my sons graduated: Max from college and Grayson from high school. I became a certi-fied grief educator. I went all-in on YouTube and my blog, taking courses on video production and social media. I hosted a child-loss support group. David and I also founded LiveLikeLibby.org, a non-profit organization dedicated to providing scholarships in our daugh-ter's memory to young dancers in financial need. I carried my sweet girl with me every step of the way, knowing that her legacy was one of kindness, caring, and unconditional love, and that I was doing my best to honor it.

I am now an author, speaker, podcast host, and YouTube person-ality in the world of grief. I've held tight to my mission of staying honest and real, and I share my good days and my bad (because I still have plenty of both). I don't sugarcoat what life is like after loss, but in my own, slightly irreverent way, I like to give others hope that grieving doesn't have to completely suck. When people ask me why I spend so much of my time talking about depressing topics like death, grief, and mental health, I simply narrate the laundry list of people that I've loved and lost in such a short span of time, and reply, "I've been through so much shit… I had to make it worth *something*."

And I believe I have.

From the scenic countryside of Lancaster County, Pennsylvania, author, speaker, and educator Brooke Carlock brings a refreshingly pragmatic and humorous approach to the often somber world of grief support. Her debut book, *Grief Sucks: But Your Life Doesn't Have To*, is far from a conventional self-help book. It is an unfiltered guide through grief, laced with the kind of candid realism only someone who's faced staggering personal loss can deliver. Beyond the written word, Brooke is a certified grief educator, the host of the "Mourning Coffee" podcast, and the face behind the YouTube channel "Grief Sucks with Brooke Carlock." You can find her at brookecarlock.org.

# THE INTERSECTION OF LOSS AND MEMORY

By Max Miller

These are the facts I know: In February of 2021, my little sister died in a car crash while I was behind the wheel. I was eighteen. Libby was ten. I had picked her up from her dance class, and a tractor trailer struck our car at a dangerous intersection while we were en route to our dad's house. That intersection had claimed other lives before my sister's; in fact, there was another fatal accident in the same location just a few months after our own.

That evening, my check engine light had come on and I was on the phone with my dad trying to figure out what to do when we were hit. The tractor trailer that hit us was traveling below the speed limit at the time, but the driver just did not have enough time to stop because I pulled out in front of him.

I only know these facts because I was told. The last thing I remember from that night is the flash of my engine light.

This is what I do remember: From the very moment I was able to retain information and make new memories again, I was reassured over and over again that it wasn't my fault, it was an accident, it could have happened to anyone, my car was having problems. I am thankful to my parents for so aggressively reassuring me of my innocence despite their own grief. It could have been tremendously easy to blame me for my sister's passing as a coping mechanism, especially since I would likely have agreed with them at the time. But because of how conscientious they were during my recovery, I don't have to battle with survivor's guilt.

I also remember my sister. When she was alive, I didn't think I was incredibly close with her, as far as siblings went. We were quite a few years apart age-wise (I was eight years older), and we didn't have a lot of common interests. When we did have something in common, we rarely spoke about it at length. I don't want to give the wrong impression—I loved my sister like I love anyone in my family.

But looking back now, I realize I miss the little stuff—the stuff that wasn't as rigid as "having a shared interest" or "having long conversations." I miss walking her home from her dance studio when I was the one that needed to pick her up. I miss hiking with my dad and listening to their conversations. I miss thinking about how good of a singer she could be if she didn't force vibrato into her voice. I miss having her around and listening to or watching her live her own life. She was far too young to die. Like any accident, her passing was incredibly unfair.

I think my grief over losing Libby started immediately after the accident, even though I wasn't completely coherent. I'm told that I asked—every thirty seconds—what had happened, why I was in the hospital, and whether Libby was okay. I had anterograde amnesia, which is characterized by being unable to form new memories. The condition rarely lasts more than twenty-four hours, which tracks with my experience. Sometime in the early morning after the accident, I woke up on the couch in our home's living room overhearing a hushed conversation between my parents.

Somehow, whether because I remembered enough to know, or because I had heard it said after the amnesia faded, I came to understand that my sister was gone. In part because of my concussion and also the amount of time that has passed since that day, it's difficult to accurately describe what thoughts were crossing my mind at the time. I do remember that, surprisingly enough (even in hindsight), I was more immediately worried about my parents than I was about myself. Sure, I had a number of stitches, a concussion, and a blank spot in my memory where the night before should have been, but my parents had just lost their only daughter. Speaking as a sibling, I cannot fathom the depths of the loss my parents sustained.

The following years after the accident were hard, for a number of reasons. I had to go back to college eventually, and when I finally did, I was so far behind that my instructor recommended dropping a few of my classes so I could focus on the ones I actually had a chance of completing. I still managed to graduate on time, which was in no small part due to the leniency and support of the people at my college.

I don't remember much about what life was like at home at the time. The days blended together into a numb soup, with the occasional seasoning of walking in on one of my parents sobbing and trying to hide it. I always wanted to tell them that it was okay, that I didn't mind and I thought it was healthy. I don't know if I ever did say it. Humans are social creatures; one of the most obvious ways this manifests is though something called "emotional contagion," a phenomenon that broadly describes peoples' moods shifting to match the moods of the people around them.

Being surrounded by people who are grieving can be as exhausting for you as it is for them because you can *feel* their grief as soon as you walk into the room. I never asked my parents to hide their grief, nor did I want them to. While I couldn't fathom its true magnitude, I could understand the weight they carried—and still carry to this day.

I didn't know what "emotional contagion" was called back then, but I know now that is why it's uncomfortable for me to be around someone who's crying. For years, as far back as I can remember, I've had a hard time crying—even when I *wanted* to cry. Crying is cathartic; it's like a dam of emotions bursting all at once and draining away, but I just can't do it often. Nowadays, the only times I usually end up crying are when I wake up from a dream.

In fact, my strongest moments of grief have to do with my dreams. I don't often remember my dreams, but a lot of the ones I do remember since the accident follow a similar formula. I'll be somewhere, doing something normal, and Libby will be there. Sometimes we'll continue doing whatever we were doing, but as soon as the dream acknowledges that my sister is there with me, the dream shifts, and I end up hugging her and crying, telling her over and over again that I'm sorry. For a long time, I didn't think I felt guilty about the accident, but I think my dreams might say otherwise.

I wish I could give people advice about guilt, but I am so far removed from my guilt that any advice I could give would be hollow. What I can and do recommend is therapy. My therapy was mandated, but I would have gone regardless. If you can find the right therapist, your life is going to be much easier going forward. A good therapist is someone to vent to, someone with whom you can talk out your feelings, someone who is *trained* to help you. While friends and family may be willing to listen to same vents and feelings, they are not trained to help you, and you cannot fully substitute talking to friends and/or family for a therapist's help.

Again, I do not want to be misunderstood; any friend or family member who is willing and able to listen is a wonder for your recovery, but you have to remember that they are people too. They can have enough of listening to you, and you have to be okay with that. My mom apologized to me every time she vented to me, and I told her every time that I was okay with it, that I wanted to hear it and to help her how I could. If you want to help someone who is grieving, one of the simplest ways is to listen.

In my experience, grief is sporadic. I'm lucky that the worst thoughts and feelings, besides those that occur in my dreams, tend to come only when I think about Libby for too long. If it gets to be too much, I can think about something else. As I understand, some people cannot do that, like my parents. They have said to me that they think about Libby every day, multiple times a day. I imagine that's common for a parent who loses a child. I don't think about Libby every day. I think about her every now and then, when my brain is idle, but it's hard to think about her without the grief creeping back in along with it.

If I'm being honest, the thing I fear the most about my grief is when my memories of the accident fully return. I've been told that it's probably not a matter of "if," but "when," and I fear that the scenarios and versions of the accident I've thought about when I let my mind wander too long will not compare to the actual memories I may or may not still have, locked away somewhere in my head. I hope they *never* return, but I choose not to live my life under the assumption that they will. I choose to live my life to the best of my ability, and remember that each day is another step away from the past.

While my sister may be gone, her memory is not, and I know my family will continue to honor her for as long as we're all around. Libby lived her life with kindness and joy. We try to do good things and make the world a better place in her name. At the time of this writing, funds have been approved to reconstruct the intersection where the accident occurred to address safety concerns. My parents are both doing much better than they were, and we're all getting by. Although I am sure we'll have more tough moments ahead, and even though the threat of my memories returning will never fully go away, I have hope that our future is bright and that we can continue with the rest of our lives, and always remember to live like Libby.

The intersection where I lost my memory and my sister changed my life forever. I'm sure that I deal with my grief differently than someone else would in the same situation. One thing I've definitely learned is that grief is very personal, and it doesn't come with a manual. I try not to judge myself too harshly and I'd offer anyone else the same advice. You never know how you will handle these types of life-changing situations until they happen to you, so just keep moving forward each day in the way that feels right for you.

Max Miller is a CAD engineer living in Lancaster County, Pennsylvania. They are a fan of video games and Dungeons & Dragons, and also enjoy the company of their partner and Mochi, their cat.

# THE GREATEST GIFT

By Bill Correll

Throughout my life, I've witnessed various shades of loss, each one adding a layer to my understanding of grief. My early childhood experiences were distant—more observational than personal. I heard stories of my maternal grandfather, who died at forty-five and left behind my nine-year-old mother and a history I'd never personally get to hear about. My grandmother passed when I was eight. I didn't attend her funeral, but I felt the effects ripple through my family. We lived in a tight-knit community, and I also observed beloved neighbors endure long illnesses and then pass. I offered my condolences to those left behind, a practice that honed my empathy.

Despite the increasing number of personal losses, I developed a method of maintaining perspective, finding solace in the notion that with each farewell, I was learning to cherish life more deeply. I diligently tended the relationships I had and made new ones, expanding my network of friends and loved ones and enriching my life with shared experiences and mutual affection.

All this changed during the COVID-19 pandemic. In a very short span of time, I lost family members, business associates, and a number of loved ones. My son-in-law's mother got very ill, went into a coma, and died. A neighbor's husband died. More relatives of mine passed. All in all, over twenty people that I knew and loved were gone in the span of twenty-four months.

During this time, my role as the level-headed, supportive corner-stone of the family was put to the test. It was particularly shattering to lose my dear aunt and my brother-in-law on the same day—on my wife's birthday. With their deaths, the foundation I had relied on for decades failed me. For the first time, I didn't reach out with cards or flowers. I didn't make memorial donations to show how much I cared. Nothing. Instead, I retreated, numbing my pain with nightly drinks, and losing touch with the relationships that had always anchored me. I didn't take good care of friends and family other than posting on a lot on Facebook. That was pretty much how I survived.

The COVID-19 pandemic affected the relationships I had with my remaining friends too. My wife, Janet, and I were friends with a dear couple named Bob and Linda, and we considered them best friends. We celebrated holidays and got together for every kind of family activity possible. We got together on weekends. We drove all over New England and had great times eating good food and look-ing at all of the sites that there are to see in the five state area. We had been doing this for more than forty years. When COVID-19 hit, that all came to a halt.

During the pandemic, Bob and my Dad were both struggling physically with their health. So I did what I could to stay in touch, seeing them both as much as possible, sharing jokes, telling stories, and just enjoying being with them! But I watched their health decline as they both spent more and more time in the hospital and in rehab from things that just happen when you're close to 80 and close to 90.

While all of this was going on, my goddaughter, Bob and Lin-da's daughter Emily, who was in remission from leukemia, had come down with what seemed like bronchitis. It ultimately landed her in the ICU for two and a half months. She was in critical condition, and they had put her in a drug-induced coma to keep her comfortable because she was having so much trouble breathing. Every day there were updates about how she was doing. We all lived with the possibility of her imminent death and dreaded the next phone call.

In addition to this, Bob and Linda had health problems of their own. Linda was diagnosed with a tumor on her brain and underwent a cranial excision to remove it. Her physical recovery was very slow and took over a year. There were also side effects with her memory going bad. As time went on and her short-term memory became worse, she had a harder time functioning on a daily basis. They wound up giving her medication to help her cope. An additional side effect was that she progressed into dementia. This went on for a year and a half. She steadily declined and it put a tremendous amount of strain on all of the relationships in the family. We felt helpless to do anything for our loved ones.

Emily finally took a turn for the better, coming out of her coma and then progressively getting better. In contrast, Linda became worse and worse and needed to have around-the-clock care at home, so they got a live-in caretaker to help with medication and feeding and all the things that were just too much for Bob to handle.

I want you to understand, Bob and I shared everything. We talked politics. We talked life. We talked about our mutual friends who were passing away because they were of a certain age. It was typical for us to talk every couple of days, and sometimes more than one time a day.

So one Friday last spring, Bob and I had a conversation after his third trip to the hospital in two months. He said, "Billy, I just came from the doctor and it's not good news. He told me that the cancer in my jaw has spread to other locations And I have to start treatment soon."

Bob had had many life-threatening episodes, including heart attacks, bypass surgery, and cancer three or four times in different parts of his body. At seventy-seven years old, he was probably about ninety pounds, but still able to get around.

I just knew that Bob world be okay yet again. I said, "Bobby, you are too ornery to die and you have never been a quitter! Now's not the time to start!"

That was our last conversation. On Sunday, I got the news that he'd had a rough night and had passed away early in the morning. I was completely unprepared.

I kept thinking, "He's going to beat this as he has so many times before."

I kept waiting for the phone to ring so I could hear his voice say, "Billy, it's a mistake. They misdiagnosed me again and I'm OK."

That call never came and I was devastated, but I couldn't cry, and I tried to contain the screaming in my head about completely nonsensical things that I couldn't understand and couldn't stop.

Once the arrangements were made and Bob was buried, I felt numb.

So now what? To cope, I devoted myself to supporting my father during his recovery in a facility following hip replacement surgery.

My stepmother MaryAnn and I regularly visited him, finding moments of connection whether he was sharing memories from his Air Force days or his childhood in Detroit. Despite a history of tension between the two of us, these interactions brought us closer, and I listened to his reflections of his life's sacrifices as a senior executive and father of six.

As his condition declined, we cherished each visit, knowing he was nearing the end. Eventually, he transitioned to hospice care, and the focus was on his comfort as we prepared for his passing. Each farewell felt like it could be our last, a poignant reminder of the finite nature of time. This went on for about a week. On the last day, we knew it was time and we stayed with him for hours, mostly so MaryAnn could hold his hand and talk to him. She still loved him so much. She said, "I still think he's very handsome. Don't you?"

We finally left the facility to get some dinner. About forty-five minutes later, my brother called and through his tears said, "He's gone."

My siblings and I went about making the arrangements and writing his obituary. Four of his children were still alive to do this, and we were all involved. There was a lot of emotional confrontation and it was clear that even though it had taken years for it to get to this point, it was now final. Everyone expressed their grief in their own way. My sister and I haven't spoken since. Maybe someday.

After the funeral, I continued my nightly routine of having "happy hour," falling asleep in my chair by 8 o'clock, and waking in the same chair the following morning. One day was pretty much like the one before.

I decided it couldn't go on.

I realized that I'd never lived my life like that before, and I had to start taking care of myself and take care of the relationships I had with my friends and family.

It took days to come out of the fog, and I appreciated all of the people who were still alive and checking in to see how I was doing.

Everything that had happened was beyond my ability to understand, and beyond my grasp to hold it all at one time. It was so much bigger than I am.

I finally decided, *I have to realize this will not change, and I also realize that I am living in dread of receiving news about the next person to die.*

What else? Who now? Why the hell should I care so much?

At some point, after a conversation with a dear friend, it just dawned on me it was time to make a choice and for me.

I stopped drinking altogether and set about refocusing myself on my lifestyle, my business, and my marriage. I decided to lose thirty pounds. I decided to go out to dinner a lot less frequently. I decided to dedicate whatever time I have left to what's really important to me. That's Janet, my daughters, my grandsons, their families, and all of my loved ones and friends.

This personal transformation has not erased the pain of my losses, but it has reshaped my response to it. I've learned that while grief is an inevitable part of life, it does not have to define it. Instead, it can be a catalyst for personal growth and renewed commitment to the values we hold dear.

For anyone struggling with similar losses, know that it is possible to find a path forward. Start with one change, one positive action. It can be as simple as cutting back on a harmful habit or as profound as reevaluating your life's priorities. Each step, no matter how small, is a step toward healing.

My journey through grief has reaffirmed my identity as a man who loves generously and lives purposefully. No matter how deep the pain we experience, the ability to give and receive love remains the greatest gift we have to offer. In sharing my story, I hope to provide not just understanding, but also hope—a reminder that even in the darkest times, we can find light.

Although I have continued to lose dear friends and loved ones, I found a way to live without the abysmal valleys of heartbreak that I experienced over the past three years.

I've had so much time to think about everything and the extent of the love that I have given the entire world. I have decided no matter how deeply it hurts to lose loved ones, being a generous, unconditionally loving man is the only true gift that I have to give to the world. That must be what I strive to accomplish.

That is who I am.

 Bill Correll is a seasoned entrepreneur and real estate investor, known for his leadership and networking skills. His career spans various manufacturing management roles. He founded PDS, Inc., and he has owned and managed multiple businesses. His real estate ventures since 1993 include over twenty properties, complemented by his role in homeowners' associations. As a committed volunteer, Bill has served as a chairman and leader on over fifteen boards, nonprofits, and commissions with a

focus on human potential. His networking acumen connects him with professionals across numerous sectors, enhancing his influence and outreach. Bill's advocacy work includes leading community groups like the Willimantic Downtown Revitalization Task Force and contributing to state-wide initiatives in Connecticut. He has supported nonprofits in improving their operations and funding stability with innovatively integrating technology into their operations. And as a certified Life and Business Coach, he assists professionals and organizations in achieving their goals, emphasizing minor yet impactful changes through his "5 percent effect" philosophy.

His podcast, "Lighting the Candle: A World that Works," recently celebrated its 160th episode, showcasing his dedication to inspirational living. Bill is passionate about empowering individuals, especially children, to live fulfilling lives. He cherishes spending time with his grandchildren, wife Janet, extended family, and networking associates.

# THEN, NOW, AND ALL OF THE TOMORROWS

By Magda Hassel

I have been on a quest to discover myself and find deep meaning and purpose for my entire life. I have always felt the need to build something great, something bigger than a typical life.

At thirty-six years old, I thought I had finally discovered myself and had my entire life planned. I had a successful career and was on my way to achieving great things in corporate America. I had married the love of my life, purchased our dream home and gotten a puppy, and was enjoying the perfect little life we were building together. Then, suddenly, I became a widow.

We had planned for a future filled with adventures, trips around the world, career successes, early retirement, and, most importantly, love. It sounds like everyone's dream. And it *was* our dream, until October 2023. October used to be a wonderful month for us, full of celebrations: my birthday, our meet-anniversary, and our wedding anniversary. Now, October carries the heaviness of my husband's death. What used to be the best month of the year has turned into a month I wish I could erase from the calendar.

I am an Eastern European woman, raised in a small town in the northeast of Romania. I had a simple, uncomplicated, and safe childhood. I grew up in a time when cell phones, laptops and the internet did not exist—a time when parents did not need to worry about leaving their kids outside unsupervised. Even though we were thirteen years apart, my childhood mirrored my husband's perfectly, which was one more thing that made our connection so in tune.

When I was growing up, my path was clearly defined by societal norms and traditions: focusing on school, getting into a good university, getting a good job, finding a husband, and then having kids. When things did not work out that way, I had my first encounter with grief. I grieved letting my family down, not living the life I thought I was supposed to, and leaving everything behind to move alone across the Atlantic to an unknown city and country. However, nothing I experienced then could prepare me for the excruciating pain of losing my wonderful husband.

I met Wyatt in October 2020, a date forever etched in my heart as the day my life changed for the best. I am convinced that God made our paths cross in the most unexpected ways and at the most unexpected time. Wyatt was my perfect match, the man that I had always dreamed of, the one I never thought I would find. From the first moment we met, our interaction was as fun, natural, and flowing as if we had known each other forever. I am so thankful he asked me out that night, and that I said yes.

Our relationship unfolded across three different continents, filled with amazing trips, thousands of hours of FaceTime calls, and deep conversations where we shared our life stories, dreams, hopes, and made plans together. We fell in love with each other instantly, and quickly realized we had found the ONE. Genesis 2:24 says, "For this reason a man shall leave his father and his mother and be joined to his wife; and they shall become one flesh" and it felt so true for us.

A couple years into our relationship, I got to say the easiest YES of my entire life and married my soulmate. It seemed like my fairytale had finally come true, and as Wyatt always said, I hit the jackpot when I met him. We got married on the same date and in the same bar that we'd met (and yes, we got married in a whisky bar). His dad officiated our marriage and we finally started the best chapter of our lives. We were excited to embark on our next chapter. But God had other plans for us. Three days after our first wedding anniversary, our fairytale came to an end.

I will never forget the call that came on a Friday evening in October and destroyed my life, my dreams, and shattered me. It tore my entire world into a million pieces and brought me to my knees, breaking my heart completely. The man who had promised to live with me until he was eighty was now gone. In the space of a few seconds, I went from being the happiest I'd ever been, to living my worst nightmare.

What came after that is a blur. I sat alone, wailing on the living room floor, and I dreaded making phone calls to let everyone know that Wyatt had died. I spent the following days planning to bring my husband back home and organizing his funeral—a funeral that was perfect and honored the beautiful soul that he was.

A couple of weeks after Wyatt's death, I returned to work. Was I ready? Definitely not. But I pushed myself into it through tears, despair, sadness, and anxiety. I didn't realize at first that work allowed me to take a short break from the grief. It helped me disconnect, at least for a moment, from the terrible loss I was experiencing. While it was the last thing that I wanted to do, my brain, my body, and my broken heart needed some respite from the overwhelming sorrow. Honestly, work kept me going.

I am still very early in my grief process, and unable to fully grasp the cruel reality of it. Sometimes it still feels like he will walk through the door and tell me it was all a bad joke. Every time I drive, I hear a voice inside my head whispering, "Hey Siri, call Wyatt Aaron Hassel." It had become such a habit to call him that my brain still thinks it is something I should be doing.

The months following the funeral have been a melting pot of emotions: shock, disbelief, anger, sadness, and depression. It's everything at once and in no specific order. One second, I am curled on the floor, crying my heart out and bargaining with God to bring him back. The next second I get angry with him for leaving me, and then I smile, remembering one of our silly inside jokes. I can never tell which feeling will shake me to my core or what moment will stir up my grief. What I am learning is that I need to allow the feelings to come in waves, experience them, and navigate through them.

The day Wyatt died, the version of myself that I'd known for my entire life died as well. I was one of the lucky ones who knew herself well and knew how she wanted to live. I didn't need to lose him to find myself. And I didn't just lose him; I also lost the person I used to be, the person my husband fell in love with. Now I am left picking up the pieces and gluing them back together to create a new version of myself. While everything may look normal on the outside, deep down, the crevasses of his loss will always be engraved in the depths of my soul.

Grief has changed me, and in a way that I don't recognize myself anymore. It has left me with a blank canvas to start over with. Initially, I believed that following in our footsteps and trying to do all the things we used to do together was what my heart needed. But I realized that forcing myself to live a life that no longer exists deepens the pain and void that Wyatt's death left in my heart.

Now, I am giving myself permission to try new things and experiences. I've stopped comparing myself to others because everyone's journey is different. Instead, I draw strength from those who have walked this path before me. My husband's death has changed how I view life and success. These days, success means getting out of bed and taking a shower, even if it's just once a week, going to work, and drinking water. It means asking for help and going to therapy. Small steps are big steps. In those very first weeks and months, I couldn't see any hope for myself. My world had ended, and all I could focus on was my pain and the loss of my husband. That is perfectly normal. My life was unequivocally altered—everything from the way I sleep, eat, work, run errands, do groceries, cook, speak, spend my time, to how I go to sleep has completely changed—and nothing feels normal anymore.

I used to be bothered by the word *healing* and got angry at everyone who said I would heal in time. How could they say that when my husband is gone forever? I used to think that healing meant going back to life before I experienced his loss. But I realized healing does not mean living the life I had planned for, because that life no longer exists and cannot be brought back. I've started to accept that healing comes with a duality I had not experienced before. It means accepting sadness while also experiencing joy. Healing is missing him but still finding ways to live my life. Healing is getting up in the morning even when I don't want to. Healing is carrying him with me and honoring his memory while my heart cries. My life will never be the same, and how could it be when my main person is not here? Healing is not straightforward, but God never promised an easy life on this side.

Faith has also played a big role in my grief journey. During my hardest moments, I have turned to God, begging Him to walk beside me and help me carry what should not be carried. Faith gives me hope that one day there will be a forever, that our love will be experienced beyond this earthly body, and that we will see each other again. I feel so grateful to God for helping me build my tribe. The new and old people who are willing to hold my hand and walk this painful path alongside me have been a true blessing.

I don't have a magic wand to wave away grief, nor the perfect recipe for coping with it. I am navigating this the best way I can, taking it one moment and one day at a time. While I cannot fathom a future without Wyatt, I am relearning to walk among the living. Sometimes I get glimpses of some sort of hope, or I feel a small fire inside me that tells me to keep fighting. I have a million things to figure out and a whole life to do that, so I am going to give myself grace and be patient. I am scared—scared of living this life without the one person who meant the world to me and loved me more than anything. But I also know that others have done this before me, so maybe I can make it as well.

People frequently ask me, *Knowing the end, would you still make the same choices and marry Wyatt?* My answer will always be a resounding YES, without hesitation. In a way, I feel lucky that this pain is ingrained in every fiber of my being because the love we shared happens once in a lifetime, and our connection transcends death. Our love is for forever, and now I just need to find a way to carry it with me until God reunites us. And I know Wyatt will be waiting for me and cheering me on to keep going.

To my dear husband: I loved you then, I love you now, and I will love you in all of the tomorrows.

Born in Romania, Magda Hassel grew up in a small -town, modest family, shaped by traditional Christian values. Magda pursued a business education, earning a master's degree in finance, and began her professional journey as an accountant.

Seeking greater challenges and opportunities, she accepted a position with an oil and gas company that relocated her to Houston, Texas. This move marked the beginning of an international career, pushing her out of the comfort zone and teaching her resilience and adaptability. Currently she serves as a Finance Director for a consumer goods company.

Outside of the her professional life, Magda is a world trav-
eler and an avid reader, always seeking self-improvement. Her personal journey took a profound turn when she found her soulmate.
However, after the devastating loss of her husband, Magda faced
the immense challenge of rebuilding her life. Experiencing grief
has been transformative, revealing her creative side and a desire to
help others through her experiences.

In the process of rediscovering herself, Magda has found a new
purpose: to keep the memory of her husband alive and to share his
story through actions and words. This mission is driving Magda to
make a meaningful impact on others, honoring his legacy while
forging her own path.

You can connect with Magda at:

Instagram: @mag_da8 and @grief_unveiled

Facebook: Magdalena Hassel and Grief Unveiled

# YOUR LEGACY PLAN
# IS THE GIFT OF A LIFETIME

*By Tina Tura Holmes*

iving my dream life, I suddenly encountered new challenges that placed me on an unfamiliar path and struggled to navigate this new path. As a funeral service professional and patient advocate, I spent more than thirty years guiding and advising families on how to make the best decisions for their end-of-life needs, offering ideas on how to effectively communicate with healthcare providers, and plan a meaningful funeral service.

Then, in the blink of an eye, I became the person who needed guidance and advice. When my partner began having unusual symptoms and then received a life-changing diagnosis, I became a hands-on caregiver. My urgent need to fix the situation became all-encompassing and exhausting as I researched and talked to others about how to get my beloved healthy again.

From the moment my partner received their diagnosis, I was unexpectedly thrust into anticipatory grief. I mourned the future we had planned and the dreams that were unfulfilled. I had witnessed people suffering from this early grief in a professional capacity, but I had never imagined that I would experience it.

How could I help my beloved move his uncooperative body, find his voice, and express his wants and needs? Who and what could help me guide him back to being the eloquent wordsmith and orator who had initially captured my heart? How could I cope with this life-changing situation? How could I become the empathetic caregiver he needed? I was consumed with fear as I witnessed his physical decline.

Remembering my education, I recalled the five stages of grief: denial, anger, bargaining, depression, and acceptance. This provided a great intellectual theory, but no solace. Trapped in my frustration at my inability to resolve our crisis, I realized how important it was to examine our situation from a broader perspective.

We often spend months and years planning for happy occasions like weddings and births, but shouldn't we also plan for the life-altering event of our own end of life? As I looked at things from a broader perspective, I discovered a solution that could help minimize the anxiety associated with what might happen to us

I confronted my worst fears and asked myself: Can I take care of my loved one at home? Can we handle the financial pressure? How can I ensure that he experiences a peaceful and fulfilling end of life?

Each scenario is painful to consider, but I can assure you that answering these questions will bring you peace, comfort, and a sense of empowerment. I have seen the devastating impact of illness leading to death and the profound effects it has on those left behind. While it is a universal truth that death is inevitable, it is also possible to minimize suffering by educating oneself, planning for the future, and sharing one's wishes with loved ones.

In mainstream American culture, concerns about aging, illness, and death are often ignored or pushed aside. As an end-of-life strategist, I have witnessed the struggle people face when they are unsure about what to do in these difficult situations. Many people wonder if they have made the right decisions because they did not take the time to ask about their loved one's desires for their end-of-life journey.

I frequently hear these questions from well-intentioned but grief-stricken family members:

- Did I honor them the way they wanted to be remembered?
- Did they want a burial or cremation?
- Did I spend too much on the service?
- Where are all their important documents: the will, insurance policy, and banking information?

We don't know what we don't know! Your first step toward taking control is learning about the process and the options available to you. Once you have done that, you can fully appreciate the benefits of having information.

To put this in perspective, imagine that you're preparing for a trip. It's common to use GPS maps while traveling to avoid getting lost and frustrated. Preparing for your legacy journey is no different than any other journey. If you're equipped with an appropriate "roadmap," you will be guided to your destination with peace of mind

The second step is to spend time creating your own end-of-life ceremony and celebration. Each person has a story, a legacy they want to create, that helps ensure their life is meaningful. Years ago, I had a first-hand encounter that changed my perspective on the positive impact of planning. A client asked me to help him plan his memorial service months before his death. He told me that he wanted to leave a gift for his family and friends. He crafted a beautiful service: the venue overlooked the mountains, he asked that his favorite music be played throughout the gathering and service, he chose his favorite foods and drinks to be shared. It was a true celebration of his life. What astonished me was that he also penned his eulogy, which was read by his best friend. During the service, laughter and tears filled the room. My client's act left a lasting impression on me about how to create a unique ceremony and reaffirmed my belief that planning mitigates the impact of loss. His story, his legacy, was a courageous and selfless act of kindness that provided solace to his wife and children..

The third step is to begin to write down the details of your life or compose your obituary. It can be a simple list: your education, career, accomplishments, community groups, interests, and hobbies. This information will help those who need to write your obituary, plan your service, or eulogy, and tell your story accurately. You can use guided tools to help you write or record your details. I believe that remembering all that you have accomplished and capturing the details of your life is healing for your soul.

Without a doubt, telling your story the way you want it to be told is a way to create a sense of comfort for yourself and those who love you. One family, who remained in denial about their well-accomplished mother's impending death, found themselves unprepared. For thirteen years, their mother was cared for in a nursing facility. After her inevitable passing, her six children struggled to remember the details of her life. As I helped them craft an obituary, with a newspaper deadline looming, there was a lot of frustration and emotional outbursts among the siblings. It was rewritten eleven times, and the stress caused divisions at a time when they needed each other. If you don't provide the information about yourself, your story and its details may be forgotten, and what you want highlighted may not be emphasized.

Although the ideas that I have shared so far involve planning for yourself, you may be tasked with overseeing someone's arrangements—as I am for my husband. I asked him to share his stories with me so I could gather the details needed to plan for his memorial. This has proven to be a healing experience and fostered an even greater connection between us. He enjoys reminiscing about his past while I diligently take notes or record him. To my amazement, I've heard some wonderful tales for the first time. I also reached out to his long-time friends to get their perspectives and insights. They enjoy telling me the stories of their adventures with my husband, and I believe it helps them cope with their anticipatory grief. Through this exercise, I can document his beautiful story and show my love and support.

Planning has provided me with solace, and the daunting questions about what I will do for my beloved are no longer so overwhelming and insurmountable. The act of creating end-of-life plans has taken the sting out of the "what ifs" and provided me with resources and options for care and comfort in our present life, while he is still with me.

The fourth crucial step in your planning process is to share your wishes with your loved ones. Make the information you have gathered available to them, along with the location of your important documents, and let them know how you would like to be remembered, what decisions should be made for you at the end of your life, and where and how you want to be laid to rest.

I encourage you to start planning now regardless of your age or health status. Death is a natural event that we all experience. Planning is a gift we can give ourselves and our loved ones. It can alleviate the burden on and the grief of those we leave behind and ensure that our personal stories are honored. Embrace the reality of mortality and take control by creating a plan that will provide peace of mind and comfort in knowing that you have prepared for the final chapter of your journey.

Tina Tursi Holmes is a leader in healthcare advocacy and funeral service education, with more than thirty years of experience in the field. She is best known for her work as the founder of Peaceful Decisions, where she provides expert guidance and resources to help individuals plan their legacy journey.

Throughout her career, Tina has been a passionate advocate for patients and their families, helping them navigate the complex emotional and logistical challenges of end-of-life planning. Her extensive knowledge of the healthcare and funeral service industries, coupled with her compassionate approach, makes her a valuable resource for anyone seeking guidance in this area.

In addition to her work with Peaceful Decisions, Tina is a sought-after subject matter expert, educator, and consultant, and regularly speaks at conferences and events across the country. She is committed to sharing her knowledge and experience with others and is known for her engaging, informative presentations and workshops.

Tina resides in Asheville, NC, with her beloved husband. They enjoy entertaining and cooking for loved ones, travel and exploring new places, and being active Toastmasters

# THE AMBIGUITY OF GRIEF

*By Connie Mae Inglis*

*"O death, where is your victory? O death, where is your sting?"*

—Paul the Apostle, The ESV Bible

I grieve a death, but not a death,
a mourning without a corpse,
a burial without a funeral,
an emptiness without a grave,
an epitaph without a gravestone.
I grieve a death, but not a death.

—Connie Mae Inglis

Time of death: October 1, 2014, 7:01 p.m. Except it wasn't. And there's the ambiguity. Yes, the time and date are correct. The final pronouncement isn't. You see, that's the day my son had his first manic episode—his first of many. And that's the day mania, later diagnosed as the extreme high pole of bipolar disorder 1, killed the son I knew and morphed him into something other.

But because there was no physical death, my loss and grief lay buried, unnamed and unacknowledged. At the time, there *was* no time to consider my own emotional angst—to process what was going on inside of me. As a mother, all my energies were spent on my son—on understanding what he was experiencing, trying to find the right diagnosis for his illness, and helping him navigate through medical assistance, medications, and psych ward life. The learning curve was steep because it was all new to me and to him.

Suddenly, I found myself crossing a bridge I *never* thought I'd cross, facing a loss I never thought I'd face. There had been no caution signs, no slow progression. No, his "death" came without warning, as it does for many with mental illness.

In today's fast-paced world, where more than one in twenty-five US adults live with a serious mental illness (https://www.cdc.gov/mentalhealth/learn/index.htm#), I know I'm not alone. There are mothers and fathers and sisters and brothers out there who have suffered similar losses. Their loved ones have been diagnosed with a serious condition, and they've been thrown into a caregiving role. But when that first psychotic episode hit my son, I did feel all alone. I was shocked and confused, hoping and believing all the while that this episode was only a one-time occurrence. That my son would somehow snap out of it. I never thought that one of my three children would be diagnosed with bipolar disorder.

It took nine months of walking this new road with my son before I began to grieve. Nine months of denial—trying to keep the reality of my loss locked up in a back room in my brain. My son had moved five hours away and worked on the road much of the time. He was working hard, staying on his meds, and making good decisions—or so I thought.

But in July of 2015, I got a phone call from his boss. My son hadn't come in to work that day and nobody knew where he was. He hadn't touched base with us or his sisters. He wasn't answering his phone. We found out later that he'd gone off his medication and was hypomanic. By the end of the week, he was homeless—living in the bush somewhere outside of Seattle. His car had broken down so he left it there. In fact, the only thing he still had, other than the clothes on his back, was his computer. Long story short, he was manic again. Thankfully, after almost a month, he contacted us to let us know he wanted to come home.

That's when I had to face my reality and grieve. Before that, I had been playing that dangerous game of pretense.

But as the episodes piled up and the number of psych ward hospitalizations increased, I had to come to terms with the truth. My son was sick. My son's brain was broken. My son, and life as I knew it with him, would never be the same again. And I grieved.

But here's the strange thing about this kind of grief—it's not typical because there's no real, physical death. And while I didn't put my son's physical body in the ground, I *did* suffer loss. I *did* have to bury other things. I buried hopes and dreams. I buried plans that would never come to fruition—both his and mine. I even buried parts of the past because the memories of who he used to be brought me too much pain.

So, I'd grieve. Process. Think I was okay. But then he would make a conspiracy theory-type comment when he stopped by. Or he'd cancel plans at the last minute because of anxiety. Or he'd confess to lying about looking for work or to spending all his money on "self-medicating." Or his psychiatrist's number would come up on the call display of my phone. And in an instant, the loss and grief would overwhelm me all over again.

Suddenly, I was on a merry-go-round that never stopped. It was not a fun, happy one from my childhood, but one more like the dark and menacing carousel described in Ray Bradbury's book *Something Wicked This Way Comes*. Around and around I'd go, sitting in a sneering clown chair as Chopin's "Funeral March" howled from the speakers. "Death but not a death. Death but not a death."

It was always worse when I wasn't prepared. I'd spin for days as I processed and grieved and then cried out to God in release. Even though my grief remained nameless, I'd learned that I couldn't shove it into a back room in my mind. When I did that, it only festered and grew, eventually breaking out to completely hijack my world.

What do you call this kind of grief? I searched for information online and in books, but found nothing—nobody named the kind of grief I was experiencing. I tried to join a grief recovery program at a local church but was told my kind of grief didn't "fit" into their workbook and sharing sessions. Out of desperation, I had to give my loss and grief a name so I started calling it perpetual because it never ended. The five or seven or however many stages of grief I'd read about proved irrelevant. Each turn of the carousel came without warning. It was exhausting!

If you have a loved one with an unpredictable mental illness like bipolar disorder or schizophrenia, I'm sure you can relate to this kind of loss.

Then finally, two years ago, I heard the term, "nonbereavement grief" in an online workshop. I sat up to listen to what this grief expert was saying. Was she talking to me? She talked about both ambiguous loss and ambiguous grief and how ambiguous grief has no exit door. Then she referenced a book by Stephanie Sarazin called *Soulbroken: A Guidebook for Your Journey Through Ambiguous Grief*. I ordered it immediately. It's Sarazin's personal story and in it she defines ambiguous grief as "grieving the loss of a loved one who is still alive," and goes on to say, "Our kind of grief is largely overlooked and most always misunderstood." The Ambiguous Grief website adds, "[it is] accompanied by a change in or death of the relationship." The website can be found here: https://www.ambiguousgrief.com/

I wanted to shout at the top of my voice, "Finally! Somebody has heard me! Somebody endorses my grief!" I felt like a weight had been lifted off my shoulders and my heart.

Have you experienced such loss and grief? The more I talk to others about my loss, the more I realize that we've all grieved nonbereavement losses, be it a move, a job change, graduation, retirement, or perhaps a more serious change like a divorce, a diagnosis of a parent with dementia, or a child with a debilitating illness. Why are we so slow or hesitant to tell others that we're sad, we're grieving, or we're struggling? For some reason, we're supposed to "suck it up" and carry on.

I have learned that there is no shame in feeling loss and sadness. There is no shame in grieving. Sorrow is part of the human condition. But, more importantly, it's what connects us all, and I think it should be celebrated. Not in a "Woooo-whooo" high-five kind of way, but in a "I get it; I'm here for you in your grief" kind of way. I know that sounds strange, but we need to be present for each other, in the good and the bad.

I have also learned how intertwined our emotions and bodies are. I have experienced headaches, back, and neck pain caused by stress and emotional angst surrounding my son's illness. I'm working on being more aware of the mind/body connection so that I stay healthy. One of the ways I heal is by being vulnerable with others. Even as I tell my story, I find healing.

I am also leaning on a faith in the Trinity God. I know him as my Creator but also as the Creator of my son, and I have to constantly give my son over to his Creator. I still have questions—I still cry out in lament to Creator God—but I know His presence. In his book *Ruthless Trust*, Brennan Manning says, "Craving clarity, we attempt to eliminate the risk of trusting God."

Oh, how I've wanted clarity as I walk this road of ambiguous grief. But ambiguity and a lack of clarity seem to go hand-in-hand in our situation. So, trusting has become part of the grieving process for me. And when I trust, I see God showing up over and over again.

A couple of years ago, I was going through a particularly sad time. I couldn't seem to get past the sadness and loss. But God didn't condemn me in my grief. Rather, in His kindness, Jesus came to me in the middle of night and offered me a word picture in a poem.

I know that sharing this poem is a vulnerable act. But I offer it to you with the hope that it will bring you some comfort and strength—and hope—in your grief.

The Visitor
An unwelcome guest
Visited me this past week.
Visited? Well, more like
Moved in.
It arrived—
With boxes stacked to the ceiling
In the living room
The dining room
The kitchen
The bedrooms
My office.
Heavy, the black marker on each box:
Names of family
Of friends
Of places and situations.
Suffocating weight
Hoarding my space, my time,
My tongue, my pen.
Hiding the windows and doors
Leaving me frozen in
Darkness.
"Come, I have much to show you," my visitor said
With a grin of self-satisfaction.
I sensed the hovering, a tyrant who
Could not be refused.
I sat and let it take over.
Sadness of the world.
Pain in relationships.

Hurt in situations.
Brokenness of humanity.
I succumbed, without navigation.
Or so I thought.

"Do not be afraid."
I turned and, in the darkness,
I see
My friend. Illuminating my
Space and time.
"Do not be afraid," he repeated.
Then I realized he had been there
The whole time. In the
Small cracks of light
Streaming between and over
The boxes;
In the narrow passageway
To the door, seemingly
Impossible to squeeze through.

But he was there,
Giving me strength to face
The sadness,
Not allowing the boxes
To strangle me.

I sat—and my friend sat with me as
The visitor opened boxes.
Spilling out memorabilia in
Space and time and rememberings.
New boxes,
The scent of pressed paper
Still lingering on the flaps.

Old boxes,
Half-crushed and duct-taped,
Smelling of crawl-spaces and mold.

"Remember well, I am here."
"Grieve well, I am here."
"Be a good steward of your pain."

Words from my friend
As together we
Considered each item.
I looked at his face. Was he
Enjoying this task?
My visitor was.
But my friend—his face was full
Of tenderness and compassion.
His eyes were red, his cheeks
Streaked with tears. He understood
This visitation of sadness.

"Do not be afraid," he said for the third time.
"I have already gone through these boxes."
His smile was gentle.
Then together,
my friend and I,
We opened more boxes.

My visitor stepped back
Into the shadows.

Then my friend invited others
To help me. As they
Arrived, the narrow entrance

Widened.
They brought food and drink,
Music and laughter.
They sat with me
And asked about this time
And that space.
The boxes began
To fall apart.

My visitor
Began to shrink, annoyed,
Though I was unaware.
And slowly,
Boxes came down
And every room began
To fill with light
And joy
And hope.

All day
The boxes
Dwindled.
And as I lay
My head on my pillow
I realized my visitor had gone
Without a good-bye.

"The visitor will be back," my friend said.
"But that's okay.
Next time there will be fewer boxes
—Or a shorter visit."
He looked at me, his eyes sparkling.
"Besides, does it matter?

I'm not going anywhere."
He laughed.
A contagious laugh
Deep and playful,
Rich with giddy joy.
I laughed too
Because, well,
I just couldn't help myself.

—Connie Mae Inglis

Connie is an award-winning author, editor, speaker, and teacher. She also hosts her own podcast, "Born on a Bridge," which focuses on building bridges of understanding and making relational connections. Her mission in her podcast and future memoir is to connect the world that knows nothing about, and often fears, mental illness, to the world of mental illness as she has lived it as a caregiver to an adult child diagnosed with bipolar disorder. She wants the world to know that in the midst of the pain and heartache, there is hope.

Connie and her husband have lived cross-culturally in Southeast Asia for the last 30+ years, dedicating their lives to working with minority language groups in Bible translation, literacy, and teaching.

Connie's greatest joy is found in her grandchildren. They fill her with love and laughter and lead her into the wonder of life. Always.

If she's not spending time with family, she is painting or hiking or camping or, if she's lucky, traveling to places she's never been, always with pen and paper in hand. Ever curious, she knows inspiration for her next poem, story, or novel could be right around the corner.

You can find Connie at: www.conniemaeinglis.ca

And connect to her podcast "Born on a Bridge" here:

https://www.conniemaeinglis.ca/media

# LOTUS RISING:
# FROM THE ASHES TO GRACE

*By Jan Jeremias*

"I am somewhere between broken and mending, and beginning and ending; I am a walking coffee blend, somewhere between bitter and sweeter—brewed from a dark roast of heartache and a light roast of love.

—Ellen Everett, *If Hearts Had Training Wheels*

It has been almost twenty-five years since my divorce, and in that time, I've spent countless hours reflecting on who I am now and how this life-altering event shaped me. The person I once was has been completely transformed; I am an entirely new being. This transformation brings to mind the bird the Phoenix. The mythical phoenix is a legendary bird that symbolizes renewal, transformation, and the cyclical nature of life. Much like the phoenix, I found myself engulfed in the flames of my own life during my divorce, a period marked by intense pain and sorrow. The phoenix, a magnificent bird, lives for centuries before it builds its own funeral pyre and is consumed by flames, only to rise anew from its ashes. In the midst of my own burning, I felt the searing pain of loss and the weight of despair, but within that inferno, a transformation was quietly unfolding. Just as the phoenix emerges reborn and renewed, I too found the strength to rise from the ashes of my past. This rebirth represents not just survival, but a profound renewal of spirit, an embracing of the cycles of life, and the indomitable journey of growth and change. The phoenix's tale now resonates deeply within me, a testament to the hope and resilience that lie within us all, guiding us to emerge stronger and more radiant from the trials we endure. For me this cycle symbolized the death of old habits, defenses, and beliefs, and the rebirth of a new, yet more authentic self. My divorce was the fire that consumed me, and from its ashes, I emerged anew.

I was with my ex-husband for fifteen years and married for eleven. One day, he came home and said, "I don't love you anymore." The next morning, he was gone. I remember we were out to dinner, sitting in a beautiful Italian restaurant when he delivered the news. I left the table, went to the restroom, and became physically ill. Even now, retelling this experience brings a wave of nausea.

In that moment, it felt as if I had died; all that I was disappeared into nothingness. Fear gripped me as I faced the impending changes. There were practical concerns: learning how to drive, managing finances, handling house repairs, and taking care of the landscaping. But more profoundly, it was the disintegration of a life I had known and cherished. I was no longer a wife. For an entire year, I couldn't even say the words "I am divorced." I avoided questions about my marital status, fearing that speaking it aloud would make it real. I had never enjoyed the single life, and suddenly, I was thrust back into that world. The dreams I had of growing old with someone, of sharing both good times and bad, were shattered. I had grown up believing in the fairy tale of a prince in shining armor, and now, that dream was gone. My entire identity had been wrapped up in him. I felt special because he had chosen me. We were quite different; he was very social, and I was quiet. All our friends were his friends, and I wasn't close to my own family. So when he left, I not only lost him, but also his family and all our friends. When he left, I felt worthless and unlovable. Some of these beliefs still linger, although many have been dismantled as I've recognized their falsity.

Divorce is a kind of death—the death of a life, a dream, shared beliefs, a relationship, and so much more. It was the death of me or who I was. Yet, unlike death, the other person is still around, and there's always the possibility they might change their mind and come back. I visualized coming home one day to find him waiting for me on the front steps, telling me it was all a mistake, that he loved me and wanted me back. I spent hours contemplating what I would say, whether I could forgive him, and if we could start again. Could I ever trust him again, or anyone else for that matter? That was a big one—could I trust anyone again?

I never went through a phase of hatred or anger. Instead, I blamed myself. There had been no conversation, no explanation, no attempt to save our relationship. He simply said, "I just want to leave; I don't want this." I am a trained scientist and I was left in a fog, trying to find a reason and answers for what had happened. I began examining every aspect of myself and our life for answers. I lived in that confused state for more than a year, barely functioning. I cried constantly and didn't eat. I worked and learned to handle the practicalities of keeping up the house or found people to help me with what needed doing, but I was not alive. I don't really remember that time. You might say I had a total breakdown. I am not sure when the breakthrough began.

I finally took a significant step forward when I began to practice forgiveness. Deep within, I knew I had to forgive my ex-husband for what he had done and the way he'd left. I also had to forgive all the people who were not there for me, who did not understand, who said unfeeling things. But most of all, I had to forgive myself for the mistakes I had made, for being overly hard on myself, for not seeing what was wrong in my marriage. I realized that at the place I was at that time and the person I was then, I was simply unable to see.

Over time, I realized that the person I was at the time when my marriage ended was unable to recognize the problems within the relationship and see what was truly wrong. Looking back now, I can clearly see the issues that existed, but I am a much wiser person now than I was back then. With the perspective and growth I've gained, I understand things I couldn't have comprehended before.

My family could not relate to me; they had never been separated from their spouses for more than a few weeks at a time, and I spent most of my time alone. My ex-husband and I didn't have human children, so my saviors and purpose became my animals. My pets gave me support, comfort, and love.

I also made progress when I began practicing gratitude. I had been taught to keep a gratitude journal during my training as a yoga practitioner and teacher, but it never worked for me. I would put the book away and forget all the things I had written down. And I always felt bad for forgetting or for not writing enough, which defeated the purpose of the practice. One day, in conversation with my mother, I mentioned that maybe I should switch to writing down one thing I was grateful for each day on a Post-it note. I began this practice, starting with my dog's name, and stuck the note on the wall in my kitchen. I continued this daily for a year. Eventually, I covered three full walls in my kitchen with Post-it notes of gratitude. Whenever life became overwhelming, I would look at those walls, reminding myself of the blessings I had.

As the years passed, I found a great therapist, attended support groups, and did a lot of work on myself. Through this journey, I realized that while I had made mistakes, so had he. Communication is everything, and its absence was the real cause of our marriage's disintegration. Growing up, I was told not to feel certain ways, and my ex-husband had also never learned how to share his feelings. Even when I did try to express myself, he would echo the words from my childhood: "You should not feel like that." As time went by, I repeatedly tried to share my emotions, but he couldn't or wouldn't understand. Because I was unheard, I became obsessed with feeling safe and secure, which led to controlling behaviors which made me feel safe and secure. After the divorce, I had to face all my emotions and with time I realized that my emotions and sensitivity were not bad; they were the reason I was so kind, caring, loving, and loyal.

I began by learning to communicate with myself. I scrutinized the words I used to describe myself, ensuring they were kind and loving. I wrote and recorded affirmations, listening to them in my own voice. This practice of self-acceptance was powerful. Yoga became a haven, a refuge. It was a community where everyone was accepted without hesitation, regardless of race, color, age, or marital status. Finding a community that supported, nourished, and challenged me was crucial.

Through yoga, I learned self-acceptance. On the mat, I was forced to confront my feelings without distraction. The physical practice helped me process emotions and understand myself better. My body became the friend and companion I needed. Yoga helped me question and dismantle my false beliefs, and I became better at articulating my feelings and being a supportive friend to others.

Being grateful for the divorce was the next step in my healing process. For a long time, I wrestled with the question, "How could I be grateful for this traumatic experience?" But as time passed, I began to see how it had shaped me into who I am today. I have evolved and transformed into a kinder, more compassionate, loving, and empathetic person. Through this journey, I came to understand that even the deepest pain can lead to profound growth.

> I am grateful for the hardship that once broke me, for it forged a strength and wisdom I never knew I possessed. Through the fire, I learned to appreciate not just the journey, but the resilience within.
>
> —Jan Jeremias

This quote encapsulates the profound realization and significant turning point in my healing journey. I am not who I was then; I am more authentic, stronger, resilient, kinder, and loving.

About a year after my ex-husband left, our divorce was finalized. Shortly after that, I became ill and was diagnosed with two brain tumors. My body, the foundation of all my support, which had been there for me through it all, had revolted against me. Once again, I was thrust into the unknown—navigating doctor's appointments, meetings with surgeons, and the realization that I might need a life-threatening operation. The doctors decided to monitor me and sent me home. I remember walking in the front door and thinking, "What do I do now?" I felt like a bomb waiting to explode. To my surprise, I hated feeling helpless. I changed everything I could regarding my health. I eliminated processed foods, began eating organic food, and purged toxins from my home—everything from household cleaners to personal care products. I started taking supplements and using essential oils. After six months, I returned for new MRIs. My hard work had paid off. One tumor was gone, and the other has remained stable for the last 20+ years. Health and wellness became my passion and profession. In a way, it was easier to work with my body than to address the emotional trauma I'd experienced. Yet, taking control of my health was a significant way to reclaim my power and feel strong again.

One of the more recent techniques that has been life-changing for me is the practice of HeartMath, where you achieve a state of Heart Coherence—a state where all the body systems, the mind, and spirit are synchronized. This brings a profound sense of calm and well-being.

By examining and transforming my self-talk, seeking supportive communities, and embracing yoga, I began to rebuild my life after my divorce and diagnosis. Each step helped me reclaim pieces of myself that were lost and discover new aspects of who I am. I found strength in vulnerability and learned to see myself with compassion and love.

My journey through grief is ongoing, but with each passing day, I continue to rise from the ashes, ever closer to achieving my true self.

To anyone reading this, take heart. Know that in the midst of your pain lies the seed of your greatest strength. Grief, though it feels all-encompassing, is but a chapter in your story, not the end. Your spirit, like the phoenix, has the power to rise, reborn and renewed, from the ashes of despair. As you navigate your journey, remember that healing is a process, often nonlinear, but always progressing toward a future where the sun rises once more. Embrace the power of forgiveness, the grace of gratitude, and the sanctuary of self-love. In this dance of vulnerability and courage, you will find your true self emerging, ever stronger, ever more beautiful. The storm will pass, and you will stand tall, a testament to the human spirit's incredible ability to rise, to heal, and to thrive.

## Practices for Healing:

- **Regulate Self-Talk:** Use words of love, compassion, and understanding when speaking to yourself. Avoid using overly critical language about your appearance, actions, or worth.

- **Affirmations:** Write and record positive affirmations. Listening to them in your own voice can be incredibly powerful.

- **Find a Community:** Surround yourself with supportive, nourishing people who challenge you to be better.

- **Yoga and Mindfulness:** Engage in practices that help you confront and process your emotions without distraction. These practices can aid in self-acceptance and emotional healing.

- **Forgiveness:** Embrace the practice of forgiving yourself and others. This can release you from the burden of resentment and allow healing to begin.

- **Gratitude:** Cultivate a daily practice of gratitude. Whether it's done through journaling or simple verbal acknowledgments, focusing on what you are thankful for can shift your perspective and bring you peace.

Jan Jeremias, a compassionate Health Coach with a career in health and wellness that spans over three decades and Bestselling Author of the book *SpOIL Your Pet: A Practical Guide to Using Essential Oils in Dogs and Cats*, shares a journey spanning three decades in health and wellness. While overcoming personal health challenges, Jan developed an integrative approach rooted in nutrition, movement, yoga, essential oils, and meditation, and created and founded Aroma Lotus Yoga. Her mission is to empower individuals on their paths to achieving vibrant health, and she extends her inclusive approach to pets. Jan offers one-on-one health coaching, private and group yoga sessions and meditations, workshops, and retreats for people and corporations. Her services can be provided online or in person, thereby allowing her to help people and their animal companions worldwide. She's not just a guide, but a heartfelt companion, supporting holistic well-being for the body, mind, and spirit.

# BEFORE AND AFTER

By Melissa Lantto

There are moments in life, their effects so great, they will cause you to organize your story in categories of "before" and "after."

**Before**

I scanned the shelves of pottery, deciding what I wanted to paint. I knew I didn't need any more knickknacks cluttering up my house. With three kids and a husband, our house was already full of enough stuff.

I stopped at a serving platter that read, "DAD, KING OF THE GRILL." Cheesy, but my husband, Chris, would love it anyway. He had just bought a new Blackstone Grill and cooked us dinner the night before, pretending to be a hibachi chef, ever the entertainer. I painted while chatting with my friends about my family's upcoming trip to Northern Michigan. I dropped the piece off to go in the kiln, planning to pick it up in a few days when we got home from our getaway.

The next morning, the kids were still sleeping, recovering from arriving at our vacation rental late the night before. Chris was heading out to visit some work clients for the day, and planned to be back to go out to dinner with us. He had started to cough a bit the previous night, so he hugged me goodbye instead of giving me his normal goodbye kiss, just in case he was catching a cold. He had Type 1 Diabetes, so he always seemed to catch viruses easily. When the kids woke up, they were excited to visit the beach down the street. Beckett, six, spent the day riding his bike, while Kailyn, thirteen, skateboarded. MaKinley, almost two years old, fought taking her nap.

Chris texted me at 2:15 p.m. saying, "Just finished, GPS has me getting back at 3:35p.m." At 4:15 p.m. I texted him back, asking, "Did you give me a bad ETA?" He did not respond. I reminded myself not to worry. Knowing Chris, he'd probably stopped somewhere on his way back and found someone he knew to talk to. It wasn't uncommon for him to find a friend, no matter where we went, and strike up a conversation.

At 4:30 p.m., my home's security camera app beeped. Upon checking my notification, I saw police officers standing on my front porch and my heart immediately sank. Something was wrong. I knew it wasn't good, and I was just hoping for the best. I frantically called the police, but they kept transferring me to different stations and told me they were busy so they would call me back. I called my mother-in-law, my parents, and Chris's best friend to help me figure out what was going on. I did not want to worry my kids until I knew what was happening, so I went outside to make the calls while they stayed inside.

An hour that seemed like an eternity later, I finally received a call from a medical examiner who asked me about Chris's medical history because she was completing his death certificate. Confused, I asked her, "Was he in a car accident?" She explained that a motorcyclist called in and said he'd seen Chris's car next to the median in the middle of the road. Chris was already dead when police arrived at the scene. They had tried to use life-saving techniques, but nothing brought him back.

I still did not understand what happened. *How does a 34-year-old just die driving?* I thought.

The examiner told me that Chris's body was already at a funeral home and they were not planning to do an autopsy. They believed that he'd had a blood sugar emergency as his blood sugar was 400 when they drew blood, however, his continuous glucose monitor read 100. I told her that did not make sense to me, that his blood sugar ran high in the 400s often and that he had experienced had diabetic ketoacidosis twice in the past, but the symptoms progressed slowly. He had texted me just before and hadn't mentioned feeling sick at all.

After hanging up, I was still in shock. I stood in the middle of the street, looking at the vacation rental, calling family to tell them. I knew my kids were safe inside and that I would have to walk in and do the hardest thing I have ever had to do: tell them that their dad just died and change their lives forever. As if our situation was straight out of a nightmare novel, a dark thunderstorm began brewing and we lost power as I walked inside to talk to my kids.

As I explained what happened, Kailyn dropped to the floor yelling "No!" and became physically ill. Beckett desperately begged me to get a rocket to fly up to get daddy back from heaven. I tried to pack up all our belongings to start the drive home and escape this nightmare. MaKinley, having no idea what was going on, just kept taking all our things out of our bags while I was trying to close them.

My phone was ringing off the hook with questions and condolences from friends and family as word spread, but I was worried about using it and draining the battery without electricity to charge it.

In the chaos, I heard a knock on the front door. It was a police officer who could not have been older than twenty. He looked at me and had no idea what to say. I guess it was his job to tell me the news, however he arrived a couple hours too late.

**After**

Picking out a casket, writing an obituary: it was not how I expected to end what was supposed to be our summer getaway. I decided that I needed to get my nails done for the funeral. Doing something that was normal for me to do felt like a necessity. I remember sitting in the manicurist's chair, feeling like I could not see anyone around me; they all looked like their bodies were blurred. At the same time, I felt like they all knew me and all knew that my husband had just died. The reality was that no one there likely did, but between sleep exhaustion and shock, realistic thinking just wasn't happening.

The morning of the funeral, I could not lift my arms up to fix my hair. I had spent the previous two days at the funeral home, greeting close to a thousand friends and family who had come to show their respects to Chris and support our family. I showed up to the church with no diaper bag, no toys, nothing to entertain my almost two year old. Sitting in the front pew, with my kids next to me, I watched MaKinley run around during the service and thought, *This is my life now, it's just me here to take care of them alone.*

While at the church, I struggled to see people. They all looked blurry again. To this day, I still don't know everyone who came and I often feel guilty that I wasn't able to personally thank each person.

I took the three paid days I was given off of work, and then went back. Friends told me, "I don't know how you do it, I wouldn't be able to get out of bed if I were you." They meant it as a compliment, but it made me feel guilty. I was forcing myself to get out of bed because I needed routine and structure to my days. I needed to focus on solving someone else's problems and not my own. I had three kids to take care of; I had no choice.

My mind started to play tricks on me. Although I had watched the casket close and lower in the ground, I thought that maybe God was just testing me and my love for Chris. Now that He saw how much I loved him, He would surely bring him back. I tried to negotiate and promise that I would love Chris with a different heart that wouldn't take small things for granted. I thought that I hadn't been thankful enough for the blessings in my life and this was my punishment.

Sleep was no escape from my mind. I dreamt nightly of Chris running away from me while I frantically chased him. The circumstances surrounding Chris's death didn't keep my mind from constantly trying to put the pieces together. With no autopsy, I had very few answers as to what exactly had happened. Chris was an organ donor and the company had disposed of his monitor, leaving me with even less clarity. I spent my nights going through all his texts and voice messages, researching what could have happened. Ultimately, I decided to hire an investigator to provide me with answers.

When I wasn't trying to investigate, I read through every text he sent me and wrote every memory I could remember down in my phone. Then I read and reread the stories I had written because I was terrified that I would forget them. The weeks following his death also entailed an enormous amount of clerical work to notify and close accounts. It felt like he was dying a little more every day as I had his phone shut off, took his name off the mortgage, and canceled each credit card account.

I was struggling, but my kids were too. For months, MaKinley ran outside every time a car pulled in our driveway because she thought it was her dad finally coming home. Kailyn wouldn't talk to me about her feelings because she said that I was already so sad, she didn't want to make me sadder. This broke me, so I started to challenge myself to go a day without crying, or only cry in the shower or when driving alone. But every time I thought I was crying quietly enough for no one to notice, I felt Beckett's little hand rest on my shoulder.

Some people process things internally; I was the opposite. Friends allowed me to tell them the same details of Chris' death again and again. They listened as I cried about the same things again and again. Friends, family, and even strangers visited us for months, stopping by with meals.

Life had been busy for many years with Chris working multiple jobs and our kids playing many sports. There were times when it felt like Chris was just out of town for work. But I will never forget that first Sunday after he died. The kids and I were home, the sun was shining in my house through the blinds, and we had no plans. I thought about how Chris would have been home, cooking us dinner with the sports channel playing on the TV. I know everyone says to expect the holidays to be the hardest, but for me it was that first Sunday.

Almost a year later, I received a call from the investigator's office. They told me that they believed Chris had most likely died of a sudden cardiac event caused by his high blood sugar and multiple other factors. I accepted this explanation and began the process of coming to peace with it. I tried to stop blaming myself for not tracking his location on his phone. I tried to stop blaming him for not taking better care of himself.

As we approached the one-year anniversary of Chris's death, I received a lot of advice from many people. Some of it was welcomed, some not. Some was good and some not so good. I hated it when people told me, "It will get easier after the first year." I was worried that meant I would be moving farther away from him and my love for him would fade. I also hated it when people said, "The second year is the hardest." At that point, I couldn't imagine feeling any worse. One of my friends, who has also experienced great loss, told me that after the first year, "It gets different." That resonated with me. Things do not get better, they do not get worse, but they get different.

## Now

Approaching three years since losing Chris, I am certainly different. Healing hasn't returned me to the person I was before. I feel like there are secrets that only people that have experienced profound loss know. I used to feel guilty spending any time away from work or taking care of my kids. But I've let go of all the perceived judgment surrounding this. I allow myself to rest and enjoy life, guilt free. I have started to stick up for myself, something I have always struggled to do and that Chris always encouraged me to do. I often wonder what Chris would think of this new me. But I also know this version of myself only exists because I love and lost Chris.

I miss not being able to share good times with him. When the kids try something new, I know he'd be so proud of them. It's been tough to accept that we will still have bad times too. There isn't some kind of "bad luck" quota that we've hit. Our kids will still get cut from sports teams and friends will betray us. But these typical lows cut deeper since we are missing such a huge part of our support system.

In many ways, we've lived our lives in fast forward. We were always busy and I was pregnant with our third baby before I turned thirty. I'm so thankful that Chris got to experience so much life with me in the short amount of time he was on this earth. But I still think about the future he didn't get to have. The plans we made that will go unlived, the daughters who won't be walked down the aisle, and the son who won't have a dad to teach him how to treat women.

I deleted all of the stories I wrote in my phone during those early days of grief after I realized that I don't need to memorize my words to remember my husband. I will never forget those times and how I felt. My kids and I talk about him daily when we are reminded of him. I also see him in my kids, in their mannerisms, friendliness, and confidence.

There are days that I feel like a strong woman and mother. Other days, I feel completely incompetent and lost. I no longer wake up every morning and think for a split second that he's still alive. But I still feel a sting in my heart every time I make a dinner reservation for four instead of five.

Almost three years ago, I was lost in my grief, trying to survive every day with a broken heart. Today, I am not only surviving but transforming and starting new ventures. Chris was part of my life for over twenty years. Being his wife is part of my identity and always will be. Now, I am honoring Chris' memory while redefining myself. I'm learning to live again, but different than before.

Melissa Lantto is the proud mother of Kailyn, Beckett, and MaKinley. She earned her master's degree and advanced graduate certificate in school and community psychology from Wayne State University, and has been working as a school psychologist since 2013. After losing her husband Chris in 2021, Melissa developed a passion for creating grief-aware schools. Melissa spends most of her time with family and friends, ensuring that happiness and fun still exist alongside grief.

# THE IMPACT OF ONE PERSON

*By Kailyn Tosto*

I didn't have an average family life when I was growing up. My parents split up when I was very young, and I don't remember them ever being together. But when I was three years old, my stepdad and biggest inspiration, Chris, came into my life. I still remember being the flower girl at my mom and Chris's wedding and the three of us pouring different colored sand into a vase to symbolize becoming a family. From then on, throughout my childhood and adolescence, Chris was my biggest supporter. Whether it was cheering me on at dance competitions, helping me with schoolwork, or making me laugh with his stupid dad jokes, he was always there.

Eventually, my mom and Chris had my little brother and sister. Even though our busy family schedule made time scarce, Chris still made me feel special by cooking me my favorite dinners and planning daddy-daughter dates for just us two. On weekdays, we woke up early, drank coffee together, and talked before school.

Chris loved taking family trips, so he often turned his work trips into vacations. The week before I started eighth grade, Chris brought my mom, siblings, and me along with him on a work trip to northern Michigan. But on the first day, he unexpectedly passed away.

From what I remember, he was supposed to be back by dinner time, but he never arrived and my mom couldn't get a hold of him. I thought it was no big deal and he was just running late. Then my mom went outside to make phone calls for what seemed like hours, leaving me inside to watch my siblings. I was mad at her for not telling me what was happening. Eventually, she came back inside and told us that Chris had passed away while driving home from complications with his Type 1 Diabetes.

At the time, his death felt so unreal. I kept thinking about how I had just told him I loved him that morning, and he had seemed perfectly fine. I never thought that was going to be my last time speaking to him. I had never experienced death so personally and I couldn't process that he was never coming back home. I dreaded falling asleep that night because I was terrified of what the next day would bring.

It's hard to remember what happened in the weeks and months following. I remember being miserable and not much else. Everything reminded me of Chris and the memories made me sad because I knew we wouldn't be making any new ones. The first time I attended a dance competition without Chris, it was hard to perform without him there. I thought a lot about the last competition he had attended and how he'd made me strawberry shortcake afterward. It just wasn't the same without him there making it extra special.

My mom recommended that I start attending a grief therapy group, but I still felt alone, like I was sinking into a fog. I felt like I couldn't share my feelings with the people around me. I didn't feel like my friends could relate or understand because they hadn't lost a parent, and I knew the rest of my family was going through the same struggle. I didn't want to upset them even more by telling them how I felt.

School was a welcome distraction. Sometimes, I would even catch myself experiencing moments of happiness. This made me feel guilty, like I was somehow betraying Chris if I wasn't miserable all the time. But when I got home from school and sports, I ended my nights by sitting in the shower and crying while the water hit me. If I didn't stay busy, it was hard to keep my mind off of all the things Chris wasn't going to be here to experience with me and it was too much to keep in.

Not long after Chris passed, a family friend sent us a card with a Bible verse on it from Psalms 34:18, which we placed on our windowsill: "The Lord is close to the brokenhearted; he rescues those whose spirits are crushed." I read that verse almost every day. It reminded me that I was not alone in my journey and filled me with a sense of hope. I leaned heavily on my faith in Jesus and his promise of eternal life to overcome my grief and heal. Even now, almost three years later, my faith is still a very important part of my life and a huge factor in my journey.

It is still hard for me to live without Chris, and I'm reminded of him every day. Since he has died, I've started high school, tried new sports, and attended school dances. I wonder what he would think of all the new things I have done. And I still think about the events he is going to miss—like my high school graduation and wedding.

Life is different without Chris. We still do a lot of the same things, like going on the same vacations, but part of our family is missing. Sometimes it's hard for me to do things that I know he loved without him there. But I realize that Chris would want me to be happy and to keep doing the things that we enjoyed doing together.

Chris always showed up and was an amazing dad to me and my siblings. He was also a supportive husband to my mom. His kindness, honesty, friendliness, and overall happiness impacted my life, and I strive to embody those same values. I have learned that I can miss Chris while also being happy and enjoying myself. With these lessons, I have been able to move forward with my life, with my faith, carrying Chris's love with me.

I have found comfort in continuing to volunteer and be involved in community events that Chris supported. Some of my favorite memories with Chris are helping him run a pizza booth at our church for many years and watching him walk with Santa at the Detroit Thanksgiving Day Parade. Seeking out ways to honor Chris by continuing to be involved in these traditions helps his legacy live on. My hope is that the impact that one person had on me will continue to positively impact many others.

 Kailyn Tosto is a high school junior, honor student, Student Council member, and National Honors Society member, in addition to being on the pompon team at her school. She has also been a competitive Irish Dancer for the last twelve years, reaching the highest competitive level one year after losing her stepdad, Chris. Kailyn has shared her grief story with hundreds of people at local fundraisers, raising money for grief programs in her school district. She is currently in the process of opening a nNonprofit oOrganization to support grieving children, in memory of Chris. She hopes that by sharing her story, other teenagers can relate and won't feel alone in their grief journeys.

# THINGS THAT MATTER

By Martie McNabb

***Reflections on Masks and Mourning in the Time of COVID-19***

I vividly remember the early whispers of spring in 2020, when the skies of Hilton Head Island held more than just the promise of the coming bloom—it held an omen named COVID-19. I had traveled there under the guise of assisting my mother pack up her rental before journeying back to Vermont. Yet unbeknownst to us, a crescendo of worry was building up around the world.

I was on the edge of a decision—to head or not to head to Florida, where friends eagerly awaited my arrival along with my camper van (affectionately named Brooklyn). However, despite their warm invitations, a gnawing feeling at the bottom of my gut whispered words of caution. I wasn't familiar with the terrain, and the idea of hopping from place to place seemed imprudent with the virus on the rise.

Pressure mounted as my mother set an ultimatum—I had to choose my next move by the morning. In a defining moment, spurred by a maternal edict and my own intuition, I steered Brooklyn away from the beckoning warmth of Florida and instead headed to the comforting presence of a friend in West Asheville, North Carolina.

Quarantine descended upon us swiftly, and I became a guardian of sorts. Donning masks and arming myself with sanitizer, I braved the outside world to procure necessities while my friend and her roommate, their lives both fraught with health concerns, stayed safely behind closed doors.

One of the most peculiar moments during that time was when my phone, once so adept at recognizing my face, failed me—rendering me a stranger behind my mask. It was a minor annoyance in the grand scheme of things, yet it marked the strangeness of our new reality.

Brooklyn was more than four walls on wheels during that time— she became my personal sanctuary, parked outside my friend's house. It served as my humble abode for ten long weeks as I assumed the role of the designated shopper, and unexpectedly, the cook. Together, my friends and I found solace in shared meals, laughter, and the support we provided to each other.

But it wasn't all moments of unity and laughter. The undercurrent of the pandemic brought with it a tide of loss. Like dominos falling, I watched as text messages and social media posts tallied up the absence of loved ones—family, friends, other connections that I held dear. They left voids that echoed across the miles.

The masks I acquired over those months became woven into the fabric of my existence, each a poignant reminder of a moment frozen in time, a story that begged to be remembered. One mask caught the whimsical essence of a gift store run by someone who had become like family. Another, crafted by a friend whose talent for illustration had given life to my Show & Tales projects, bore an image that was the very essence of Brooklyn, where a part of my identity lay.

Living through those times was like walking a path littered with both gemstones and thorns, each step a testament to personal resilience and the power that comes with belonging to a community, no matter how distanced we were forced to become.

These masks I hold, the memories they represent, are more than just a part of the past. They've etched themselves into my being, my story—a narrative interwoven with threads of loss, courage, and the undeniable truth that even the simplest objects can become vessels of profound meaning.

So, if you ever come across a camper van named Brooklyn, with a woman who carries stories as numerous as the stars in the sky, take a moment to listen. For within every crease of her collected masks, there rests a lesson in courage, a whisper of hope, and the comforting knowledge that, in the end, we all have Things & Stories that matter.

### Honoring Loss and Legacy: A Journey Through Grief and Memory

In the winter dawn of 2020, I stood where beginnings and endings collide, not knowing how deeply the year would etch its story onto my soul.

My father, my steadfast oak, at last succumbed to the passage of time, his leaves falling gracefully just as the world outside prepared to hibernate in the face of something unseen. We honored him, a celebration of life amid the silence that was about to fall.

That fall, just before the tapestry of grief and stillness of THAT spring, before the world shut down due to the pandemic, Keekee entered the scene. She was like a gust of wind in a quiet forest, invigorating and full of purpose. Her laughter was a beacon in the dimness. Her mission? To uplift veterans who'd been forgotten. Together, we conceived a project, a lifeline, threaded with hope and the stories of the Things That Matter for Soldiers, Sailors, and Civilians.

A token of gratitude, a simple yellow postcard from Keekee, floated into my life, a sunny reminder of the goodness fluttering in human hearts…her simple *thank you* glowed like a miniature sun amidst my trinkets. It was to be a lasting memento of a burgeoning friendship, one I never imagined would be but a fleeting chapter.

The narrative of love and remembrance wove through the fabric of a workshop by artist Caito Stewart via "Let's Reimagine," a sanctuary for souls navigating the twilight dance of life and death. There, the idea of Ghost Kites, carrying the names of those who have died, inspired me to embrace a ritual of honor using paper leaves as the canvas for the names of lost loved ones.

The paper leaves, though, lay blank for three years, heavy with unshed goodbyes.

It was during a retreat, in the warm embrace of Mexico, that my grief story found its home.

With gentle hands, I wrote twenty-five names upon the leaves I had carried—the leaves that had waited patiently to be kissed by ink and carried by flames. As the bonfire licked the night sky, I released the leaves, speaking their names, each one taking a piece of grief, illuminating the darkness with sparks of gratitude, and sending love and memories swirling into the stars.

And so, my tale is a mosaic of love, family, and friendship, and the eternal cycle of endings and beginnings.

It's a story of how sometimes, the smallest objects hold the greatest stories, and how letting go isn't about forgetting—it's about freeing one's heart to carry those we've lost, not as a burden, but as a guiding light for the paths we've yet to tread.

It reminds us that in this vast universe, what truly matters are the connections we make, the love we share, and the rituals that allow us to say, "You mattered. You will always matter."

Alan McNabb
Larry
Elaine
Meredith
KeeKee
Pete
Yolanda
Gordon
Rich
Sue
Marty
Tessie
Louis
Liz
Waldo
Elizabeth
Carmelo
Len
William

Angela
Regina
Robin
Sharon
Glen
Patrick

Grief is like a storm; always look for the horizon and gather your trusty crew. You will make it through together… knowing another storm will whip up at any moment. Touch something they touched and know you are not alone.

 Martie sold her apartment in Brooklyn 6+ years ago and hit the road in her twenty-one-foot camp-ervan (named Brooklyn) to host story-sharing gatherings & interactive art/history exhibitions for individuals, families & organizations all over the country. She's on a mission to build deeper connections, community, and legacy through the stories of the Things that Matter. She's been written about in the Wall Street Journal and featured in three books. She splits her time between her wife and mom-in-law in Albuquerque and her mom in Vermont. When she can, she meets her wife, their marriage 30+ years in the making, on the dance floor where they met a lifetime ago. Check out her show *Things That Matter with Martie McNabb* on YouTube and anywhere you listen to podcasts. She's launching a series of multi-author books all about the Things that Matter in the fall of 2024.

# PRECIOUS TIME

*By Carin Mikos*

In the quiet, often overlooked moments that occur in the corridors of hospitals, I found my calling. I stumbled upon a world that teetered on the fragile line between life and death when I was a nursing student assigned to the oncology floor. It was here, in sterile rooms filled with the muted whispers of nurses, that I discovered a piece of my heart. I realized that there exists a sacred space where one can dance gracefully with both life and death. My epiphany did not come all at once, but rather through the accumulated experiences and connections I made with those facing their final moments.

One of my patients, Tim, with his quiet strength and resilience, was my inaugural guide into the deeply personal journey that the twilight of life represents. He was on the oncology floor, fighting a type of blood cancer, and was getting weaker and weaker. He would go home and would only be there for several days at the most. He had tried all the treatments. This went on for several months. Eventually, there was nothing left to do. With kind eyes that spoke of a life lived fully and a weary smile that hinted at acceptance of his fate, he invited me into his inner sanctum with surprising ease and grace. This was a man who understood the gravity of his situation, yet he chose to embrace each day with an openness that was both humbling and inspiring.

Our conversations unfolded in quiet moments that bookended the bustling activity of my day-to-day responsibilities. These stolen pockets of time—before the day officially began, sandwiched between the duties of my shifts, and in the reflective calm as day eased into night—were not filled with the somber tones of mortality, but were vibrant with the essence of living. Because of Tim, I came to understand the significance of the seemingly mundane: the dreams that dance on the edge of our consciousness, waiting for the right moment to be realized.

He spoke of his simple desires with a palpable longing—the dreams of wandering through distant lands, the simple joy of family gatherings and shared stories around the dinner table on lazy Sunday afternoons, and the innocent wish to sculpt sandcastles on a beach, surrounded by the laughter of his grandchildren and feeling the warmth of the sun as it set. Our conversations were not about dying; they were affirmations of life, of the small moments that keep us tethered to this world.

The task of writing letters to Tim's family was one I approached with a reverence that belied the simplicity of putting pen to paper. We chose each word with care, each sentence becoming a fragile thread that wove together vibrant hues of memories, subtle shades of hopes yet to be realized, and whispers of unspoken farewells. A letter to ten different people. Some family, some good friends. This act of finality, encapsulating his life into the confines of a letter, was a poignant reminder of the indelible marks we leave on the hearts of those we love.

The moment I learned of Tim's peaceful passing, surrounded by the love of his family, was etched with a mix of sorrow and serenity. It was then that I felt an undeniable pull towards the realm he had so gently introduced me to—a hallowed place where the dichotomy of love and loss coalesces into a singular, heartfelt truth. It was in saying goodbye to Tim that I fully grasped the beauty and pain intertwined in life's final chapter, when every moment is a gift.

After Tim's passing, I delved into the world of nursing, seeking the knowledge, understanding, and skills necessary to support others as they navigated life's health challenges. I worked in the emergency room, the burn unit, and intensive care unit where people fought for their lives. My journey was not just about acquiring the technical know-how to care for others, but also about personal transformation. I came to see death not as an enemy to be feared, but as a natural, intrinsic part of the fabric of life. My experiences on the oncology floor, in the trauma bay, and in the intensive care unit reshaped my cultural, religious, and familiar perceptions around death and dying. They taught me to cherish the fleeting moments in the gaps and to approach the end with grace, compassion, and a smidge of curiosity.

I eventually left the world of clinical nursing and almost missed the opportunity to be a home care nurse. I found hospice homecare during the COVID-19 pandemic. It was here, in patients' living rooms and around their kitchen tables and sitting on their couches that I fell in love with people again. The years of front- line nursing and struggle to meet the high physical and emotional demands of that career had forged a wedge between me and people.

The first time I stepped into the home of a new patient, I was greeted by a sound that immediately tugged memories from the depths of my experience—the labored breaths of someone fighting for each inhalation. This was Kathy's battle, underscored by the weary, yet steadfast, gaze of her husband, Don, who stood sentinel by her side. Amidst this silent storm, the comforting aroma of chicken soup drifted from the kitchen, a stark contrast to the palpable sense of worry that filled the room.

As I approached Kathy, the signs that she was waiting to pass were unmistakable. Her struggle to drag in each breath spoke volumes about the amount of pain she was in, and it was clear what needed to be done to offer her some semblance of comfort. Morphine was the key to easing her path, a gentle reprieve in the face of her relentless struggle for air. Turning to Don, I broached the subject, and noted the hesitation that flickered across his face—a mix of uncertainty and fear, and perhaps, a silent plea for more time..

Sensing the need for privacy and a moment of candor away from the immediate weight of Kathy's suffering, I suggested we retreat to the kitchen. There, we sat down at the table that looked as though it had been the stage for countless conversations. It was here, in the heart of their home, that I asked Don for permission to speak openly and address the unspoken truths that hung between us.

As tears welled in his eyes, a testament to the love and pain interwoven in the fabric of his being, Don nodded. In that moment of vulnerability, I gently laid bare the reality we faced: Kathy's time was ending, and our immediate task was to ensure her comfort and make her remaining time as peaceful as possible. Our conversation was not just about practicalities; it was a shared acknowledgment of his love and impending loss, a delicate dance of holding on and letting go.

Delving deeper into the complexities of their situation, I addressed Don's reluctance about using morphine. His concerns were multifaceted, rooted not only in fears of its potency and potential side effects, but also in a deeply personal tragedy. Don revealed to me that they'd lost their son to an overdose just three months prior—the tragedy had left Kathy barely able to eat, let alone muster the strength to face her dwindling days. The rawness of Don's pain was tangible. Tears traced unbidden paths down his cheeks.

In that moment of shared sorrow, I reached out, offering the simple comfort of a gentle handhold. I assured him that although the path ahead was difficult, he wouldn't have to navigate it alone. I was there to guide them through each step. I talked about the purpose and proper administration of morphine—not as a harbinger of the end but as a balm to ease Kathy's breathing, to offer her moments of respite during her struggle.

With patience and care, I demonstrated how to prepare and administer the dosage, framing it as an opportunity for him to play a crucial role in Kathy's comfort. I attempted to lighten the mood with a comment about how I was quickly to be the hero or a fool. We shared a laugh and I felt trust spring up between us.

After administering the first dose to Kathy, a concentrated liquid designed to be absorbed under the tongue, we stood by her side, united in silent anticipation. The weight of the moment was palpable, a collective holding of breath as we awaited the result. Miraculously, within minutes, Kathy's labored breathing eased, and she was able to speak whispered words of gratitude. The change was marked by a smile that lit up her face. It was a moment of connection and an example of the power of compassion and medical care to bring solace even in the darkest of times.

Don, again with tears in his eyes, turned toward Kathy, engaging her in conversation about the simple pleasures of life—their grandchildren, the comforting aroma of the soup, the familiar favorite of grilled cheese. It was a conversation emblematic of their sixty-two years of shared life, but imbued with an extraordinary significance as they navigated the end of their journey together.

Kathy's final days unfolded in a cocoon of familial love and culminated in her peaceful passing. Her departure was graced with dignity, a serene finale to an odyssey of deep connections, mutual support, and shared experiences. And it highlighted that her journey was not merely ending, but had reached fulfillment, supported by the unwavering love at its foundation.

This heartfelt experience serves as a profound reflection on the intricate dance of love and loss, the critical role of compassionate caregiving, and the power of human connection that prevails even as we navigate the inevitable passage from life to death. Even amid the sorrow we feel, there is beauty in the connections we forge, the care we provide, and the memories we create together. The legacy of love Kathy left behind should set an example for all of us.

I hope this story imparts several key takeaways for all of us. It reinforces the value of approaching the end-of-life journey with dignity and encouraging an open embrace of the complexities of human emotions. It highlights the indispensable role of compassionate care and the difference it can make in the final days of a loved one's life. Most importantly, it reinforces the enduring power of love and relationships, serving as a reminder that even in the face of loss, we can bring comfort, peace, and a sense of completion to those we hold dear. Let us carry forward the lesson of Kathy and Tim's lives and her passing—a reminder to cherish every moment, love deeply, and face life's transitions with grace and empathy.

 Carin Mikos has twenty-seven years of experience as a registered nurse and has been an end-of-life specialist for the past four years. She is the creator of The Quietus House, a concierge service dedicated to supporting folks at the end of their lives.

# PERFECTLY BROKEN

By Danielle Miller

This is just one story. But it's my story and reflection on the last twenty years. My grief is a little different. I lost myself.

I was your all-American girl. I was sixteen years old and had a good life despite coming from a divorced family. I was a cheerleader, peer mediator, captain of the volleyball team, and on the student council. I was excelling, thriving, and happy.

On Labor Day weekend, just as I was starting my junior year of high school, we went to my Grandma Roxy's. Like any other weekend, it was days of nonstop fun on the lake and evenings of singing around the bonfire and telling funny and scary stories with my brother, cousins, our friends, and older family friends. We fell asleep looking at the stars and listening to the waves hit the shore. Everything was relaxed and free. It was my happy place.

Little did I know that on this particular weekend I would be raped, by not one but two forty-year-old men. I had always been a girl who spoke up for herself. However, in that moment, I was paralyzed and numb. I could not even speak, let alone move. It was like everything I had ever learned left my body, and I felt lifeless as they took their turns having their way with me. How could a friend of my family, someone I'd trusted—that my grandparents and parents trusted—do that to me? I'd known them my entire life.

Once I could breathe again and my soul came back to reality, I ran back to my grandma's. My brother found me crying at the side of the house, so I told him because he could clearly tell there was something really wrong. Once I told him, he ran to tell our grandma. She then called the police, not even knowing what had happened, just that my brother said Danielle was raped by two said names. I didn't know that by telling, I'd be facing so much more. I started questioning myself. Did I do something to provoke it? What had I done that would have caused anyone—let alone a family friend—to do that to me? Why me? Could I have done anything different to change that night? I had always believed that God does not give you more than you can handle, so maybe this was my obstacle to overcome in life. As strong as I thought I was at the time, I was also so weak. How could I go on living life on life's terms when the people I thought I could trust used me at their disposal? How was I supposed to live, reeling in the turmoil of what they had done to me, while they were still out there living their everyday lives?

That was just the start. I still had to go to school and embody that wholesome, involved girl I used to be. Could I go to class? Could I stand it if anyone bumped into me in a hallway? What about my principal who was a male? Did he have to know? Should he know? It was a lot to process as a very hormonal sixteen-year-old girl. At that point, I didn't want to be alone and even though I gathered the strength to put on sweats and go to school each morning, it wasn't long before the nightmares set in. I relived that terrible night over and over again.

My grades started slipping, and it was like I'd forgotten everything I knew how to do. I didn't sign back up for cheerleading, and quit all the things that at that time made me Danielle. It felt like I was an infant who relied on their parent for everything all over again. One of the hardest things was losing my ability to trust anyone other than my mom and grandma. They were both there every step of the way.

My mom tried to make sure I got all the help I needed. She let me sleep in and go to school late because my dreams haunted me. My entire existence had been violated and my experience haunted every aspect of my life. If someone I knew and trusted could hurt me like that, then how could I expect anyone to help me deal with what happened? With a lot of positive encouragement and the promise of always having someone nearby to help me feel safe, I finally agreed to counseling. But I kept asking, Was I safe? Was I safe from myself?

Eventually, I got on the road to start my healing process. That led to one-on-one talks with my therapist, the school therapist, and the team they had built to communicate with each other to make sure I always felt safe. Once I built up enough confidence, I even entered a recovery house where boys and girls my age who had experienced trauma lived together and built a foundation from which we could start trusting a little. That helped me start to realize not everyone is evil.

But as much as I wanted to heal, I couldn't forget. I still had to endure the legal part of it. And if the rape kits, blood test, and pills weren't enough, I still had to answer questions from attorneys and police officers and sit in a room without my support system, all the while feeling like I was the one who had done something wrong. I was just reliving the event all over again—expecting something to happen to get some sort of justice.

All of this contributed to a turn for the worse and my self-destruction. I started drinking on school nights, ignoring or putting little effort into schoolwork, and ultimately forgetting who I was and losing respect for myself. I lost myself. You can have a huge support system, but if you don't take the time to process your trauma you can still lose it all. I was working through mine, but even though I felt like I had a hold on it, I was starting to spiral more and more out of control. I started numbing myself just to get by. I suffered from PTSD and anxiety attacks that still affect me today. It got so bad that I was put on medication so I could get through my senior year and graduate. However, at the end of the day, it was a Band-Aid. I was still in complete destruction mode. As long as I seemed okay on the outside all would be okay. I was not okay though. I was still facing demons I didn't know I had!

After high school, I thought I'd had enough guidance and therapy to keep living life. Instead of starting college, I got a job as a shot girl in a strip club. I was being noticed, but I was still so lost that I didn't realize it was not the kind of attention I needed. I learned how to manipulate and deceive men for my own personal gain. I moved away from home, out of the only place I knew how to be safe, and rented my own condo and got a new car. For the first time, I felt like I'd found the body I knew to be mine and everything I had once lost. I thought I'd regained the confidence I had lost. I felt in control again.

I was really starting to love the money I was making, so I started putting in for more shifts. But the long late nights at the bar eventually started to catch up with me and I was tired all the time. One night in the bathroom at work, a coworker offered me a pick-me-up to get through the rest of my shift. It was not long before those pick-me-ups became a nightly habit. Once again, I was ashamed of the person I had become, and there was an emptiness inside me. I went back to the resources I was given before I called my mom and told her I needed to come back home. She got me a job at one of our local casinos. I also started cosmetology school and got deep into therapy. It was there I realized that I was still living with all of my past trauma. I needed to start from the beginning of my self-destructive behaviors in order to heal.

You're not a target just because you're a pretty face. You're not a target just because some people don't know how to control their impulses. But after experiencing something like that, you can either be a survivor or a victim. Even though I still struggle with my demons, today I am officially able to say that I am a survivor.

I'm just a regular girl from Detroit, Michigan, and today I'm a stay-at-home mom. I feel like I've jumped through every obstacle that life has thrown at me (good or bad). They have run the gamut—from being sexually assaulted to dealing with addiction to losing my kids because of my addiction. After years of self-shame and humiliation, I am finally able to write about these things, all the while hoping that by sharing the darkest parts of it all, I can help anyone else who is suffering in silence.

# TILL DEATH DO US PART:
## Lessons of Love & Loss

By Kate Mollison

At the tender age of nine, I was already an expert funeral attendee. I clearly remember multiple instances standing in a crowded room with a dead body while wearing uncomfortable clothes and shoes that made my feet hurt. The concept of death and the funeral process was never really explained to me, and I'm not entirely sure I understood what "grief" was at that age, but that was the vernacular used by all the grownups to explain the immense sadness and heaviness in the air.

By the time I was twenty-one, I had no living grandparents, no aunts, no uncles, and I had also lost a handful of teachers and close friends. Given all that exposure to loss, I would have considered myself a grief aficionado … but even with all of that practice, I still wouldn't truly know the wrath of grief until I experienced a loss that completely unraveled me.

I was tragically and unexpectedly widowed at the age of thirty-two. I had been married to my soulmate for almost ten years and I can honestly say we had it all… we had the dream house, two beautiful children, and we were settling into a life that was beyond my wildest dreams.

It was all taken away from me in the blink of an eye. In November of 2020, just two days before Thanksgiving, Craig suffered from a pulmonary embolism as a result of egregious medical negligence.

Craig's death was sudden, but our journey to that endpoint was not. After experiencing an orthopedic injury over that summer, we dealt with months of missteps and mishandling by multiple individuals. After physical therapy "corrected" the initial issue, Craig began to experience numbness and weakness in his legs with excruciating and debilitating pain in his lower back. We pleaded with the orthopedic doctor, questioning his abrupt change in pain levels and mobility, but were met with dismissiveness and instructed to stay the course. So we did. We scheduled routine follow-up appointments, tried every over-the-counter pain reliever, and Craig diligently attended more physical therapy, even on the days he fell down the stairs because his leg went numb and gave out. I watched for three months as he became less mobile and more fatigued.

The dance between the unwitting orthopedic doctor and Craig's diminishing capacity came to a head when he abruptly went completely numb from the waist down. What could have been taken care of with simple imaging and minimal remediation turned into a wild goose chase of symptomatic interventions that led to urgent measures. On a cold rainy night, November 11, my children watched their father leave our home via ambulance for what we didn't know would be the last time.

We spent over twenty-four hours in the emergency department, with Craig enduring a barrage of invasive testing to try and figure out why he had gone numb. Ultimately it was deemed necessary that he have spinal surgery. Once Craig had surgery, it was two weeks of juggling my full-time job, my young children, and a husband in the ICU during covid. Finally, we thought we saw light at the end of the tunnel. Craig was to be discharged to a rehabilitation facility where he would work on recovering. We were relieved! But only three days after arriving at the hospital for special care, Craig coded.

What we learned later on is that there were several key points of negligence from the orthopedic treatment as well as during the surgical after-care that ultimately contributed to his death. The autopsy even says so.

Due to COVID-19 restrictions, I hadn't laid eyes on Craig for about a week as the rehab hospital had a different visitation policy than the hospital where he'd had surgery. We had spoken on the phone the night before, and he had video called the kids a few days prior, but I had not hugged my husband in almost a month.

The morning of Craig's death started like every other morning had over the past four months, and I was excited because I was able to schedule a surprise visit for his birthday the following day. Then my phone rang and my world came crashing down. I raced to the hospital, beating the ambulance there, so they stuck me in a little green room for what felt like an eternity. The social worker, not for lack of trying, said all the wrong things as I sat there trying to convince myself that he was ok. Finally, they told me I can see him, but no one prepared me for what I was about to witness. The last ten minutes of Craig's life are vividly seared into my mind.

The doctor pushes open the curtain in the trauma bay, and comes out from behind it. I can see her mouth moving, but I don't hear her words, everything sounds like I'm underwater. All I see is Craig. He's naked, intubated, on a backboard with a neck collar, and a chest compression machine violently forcing his body to perform in a way it doesn't want to...

I scream and fall to the floor. This has to be a terrible dream—it's not possible that this is real. He and I had just spoken not twelve hours before. The doctor tells me that they've exhausted all options, and even if they can get his heart beating again, there won't be brain activity. His brain had been without oxygen for over thirty minutes. I crawled across the hospital floor and clung to his leg tightly, begging him to come back to me, but it was no use. "Ten forty-three, time of death." Those words rang in the air like a church bell.

As the smoke cleared and the room emptied, I was left with a dead husband and my racing thoughts. I sat with Craig, trying to wrap my head around what had happened, as I watched his skin slowly turn a purplish gray. I remember asking myself, "What the hell am I supposed to do now?!"

I had no idea what to expect in the coming days, weeks, months, or years, but I knew the moment he died, I died too. The version of me that had existed could no longer continue. But out of all the things that I didn't (and couldn't) anticipate, the most surprising was the answer Craig gave me to my repetitious question.

Grief is not the beautiful, emotional epilogue we're disingenuously force-fed in movies and on TV. It's ugly, it's raw, and it's a prison sentence—until you decide that it's not. The truth of the matter is, I struggled from time to time to get myself going. Sometimes it was day-by-day, other times it was from minute-to-minute. I had to stop approaching grief like a Rubik's Cube. This is not something to be solved. To survive grief, you must first decide to not let it hold you hostage. As easy as that may sound, it is a very intentional choice.

I personally hate the phoenix metaphor of rising from the ashes; like, I'm supposed to wear this tragedy like some badge of honor? No thanks. But it is true that to a certain degree, we must rise above our tragedy and choose to live. Therein lies the answer I wasn't expecting. It's not about survival. Grief has the beauty to be fuel for the second life we are gifted. To move forward with grief, we must make the difficult choice to continue living on in their absence. It took me a bit to understand this. Initially, I found myself dismissing this concept, as it felt like just another platitude. But I quickly learned that the harder I swam against the current of grief, the mightier its wrath.

Transparently, it took more than just losing Craig to learn this. I had to lose so much more. Grief is incredibly isolating; I not only lost my spouse, but my co-parent, best friend, confidant, lover, co-bread-winner... the very foundation of everything I knew was eroded. My world was suddenly upside down, my security was shaken, my social circle had dissipated and I was left to figure it all out on my own. I was still working and trying to be a mom and hold everything together (emotionally and financially), all while still processing everything that had happened. Beyond losing those intangibles, we endured the loss of our home, and the loss of a lengthy wrongful death suit.

In spite of everything I lost, I gained perspective. I knew the moment Craig died that my life would be changed forever, but I didn't know how. I found strength and resilience that I didn't know was possible. I found a version of myself that I never knew existed. (A version that Craig would be so very proud of.) I found my priorities. I can easily discern where my time is best spent because I have the painful reality of knowing that time is gift. I have found my purpose. I have taken my experience and alchemized it, garnishing formal learnings so I can better identify gaps in services for those experiencing grief. I can assess the landscape from a place of experience to advocate for change.

I am light-years away from the woman I was on that November morning. I have traveled what feels like 10,000 miles emotionally. That's not to say I don't still have bad days, because I do. At the time of writing this, I'm just three years out from Craig's death, and I am still learning to navigate this journey as my grief continues to change and evolve.

Ultimately, I can't change that Craig died... It is a cold hard fact that when spoken out loud, tastes like vinegar. It would be very easy to wallow in my grief and become consumed by it, but that would be a disservice to the incredible man that I was lucky enough to call my husband. Instead, I can appreciate that the real gift and legacy Craig leaves behind is the power of perspective.

In honor of Craig, I choose to embrace the power that can be found in grief. To reminisce and lovingly remember our time together, and to share what I have gone through, so I may foster healing and awareness for others.

Love you 3,000, Craig.

Kate Mollison is a certified grief coach who uses a unique approach to promote awareness around the importance of grief. Using her own experiences as a widow, Kate adds a personal touch to an otherwise isolating and difficult topic. She is the founder and operator of *On Tuesdays We Wear Black*, a consulting company, working as a grief and bereavement specialist, where she focuses on helping others understand the connection between "grief" and "bereavement". Kate has several years' experience as a clinical case manager and as a certified "Playmaker," she uses a modality that helps people unlock joy and find peace and meaning again after loss. By educating both individuals and businesses about the importance of grief integration, she provides education that fosters visibility and support.

# HEALING THROUGH WORDS

By Dan Older

**Sibling Island**

Welcome to Sibling Island.
No tickets needed here
just a desire to get help
and a reason to want to live.

It's so full of love
Full of compassion
An experience like no other
Long nights for sure

There's the personal
Home movie theater
Where we watch our
Favorite shows

Some are crazy and fun
Some home videos too

A trip down memory lane
As we share in our past

The huge kitchen with chefs
Where meals are cooked
Whenever the desire comes
A snack, a dessert, a comfort food

The baking of a cake
For your sibling's birthday
Happy memories shared
A few tears maybe shed

The beautiful family room
With high ceilings and chandeliers
Huge picture window overlooking
Lake Love and its forest beyond

Furniture fit to each need
Recliners to sofas
Anything you can imagine
A beanbag brings back the memories

The lights can be dimmed
The fireplace lit
Hours of talking
No time limit set

The wraparound deck
Each side a new sight
Beauty beyond words
And that's just the house

The nature trails
With flowers from
All around the world
Your senses on overload

You just stop and breathe it in
You smile and relax
My, what a place
This island provides

Hiking, biking, swimming, and motorsports
A place to let off steam
When emotions decide
They want to take center stage

You are never alone
Someone always nearby
A safe place to be
Love and peace so sweet

You hate the reason you're here
Why it happened you'll never know
But since coming here
You don't want to be anyplace else

Here, you don't have to be strong
Here, you can break down
Here, you are accepted
Here, love really wins

If you could've skipped the pain
And gotten here another way
Maybe together you could've came
And experienced it together

But that's not what happened
So you accept this life change

The Island is a place in your mind
But it's also where you meet in real life

The island is all around us
If we just look really hard
Maybe it's in a message check in
A "Hey, how are you doing"

You know it's in our zooms
As we get to see and hear each other
The island is everywhere
And it's what you make of it
 It's a place of love
It's a place of acceptance
Don't ever lose hope
We're always just a message away

The Island isn't complete
Without all of us together
So hold on tight
Let the adventures begin
The Puzzle of Life

A beautiful puzzle
Pieces all there
It's your favorite picture
You look at it all the time

There you are smiling
Glorious sunset behind you

Sky dancing with multiple colors
Your oranges, reds, pinks and violets

You're on the beach
It's so peaceful
Your whole family is there
Everything is perfect

Like a thief in the night
Tragedy strikes
The puzzle is broken
Into a thousand pieces

Chaos ensues as you
Try not to panic
Oh my word what just happened
All was just right in the world

The pieces are spread out
You try to place them back
But you're just too confused
No picture to copy from

You throw it in the box
Frustration, sadness, fear
It all sets in
You're lost, what's next

How will you recover
When will you recover
You pull the box back out
And spread out the pieces

You're reminded right then
Like the tragedy struck yesterday
Thousands of pieces
Just staring back at you

You start with the corners
And then find the edges
The framework is done
Still a lot of missing pieces

What's this right here
Where does this piece go
Start to get discouraged
Can I really get this done

Piece by piece you get it done
You're coming to the end
A few more to go
But then you panic again

Will the puzzle be complete
Will the hole ever be replaced
What will fill its place
Or should I even try

But then you see the final
Piece and put it in its place
The excitement that you've done it
The puzzle back together again

But as you look at that spot
That spot that worried you so

It's not gone forever
It's still right there

It's just a little faded now
But tragedy did not win
For in the end
When you see them again

The color will return
The beauty returns
Your life will be complete
So too will the puzzle of life

**Who Are You?**
Who am I you may ask
Well, sit right there
I will tell you
Exactly who I am

I'm the great one
The all powerful
All-consuming one
I enter your life and don't leave

I bring sadness and heartache
I strike like a Lion
I hide very well
Only to devour you

Stress and anxiety they
Come along with me

I make you question your
Thoughts and your very words

I put tension on your
Most closest relationships
Trust and fear they overtake
Your very being

I affect your job
I affect your mood
I affect how you eat
I affect what you drink

I push you to say crazy things
I push you to believe
That if you are not alone
You most certainly feel like it

I make Goliath look small
And yourself like an ant
I'm larger than life
But you can't even see me

Like a chameleon I blend in
And like a mouse
I take bits of you at a time
Until it's too late

You can win many of our battles
But the war you will not win
I cannot be defeated
We're attached at the hip

They call me Grief
I'm the meanest of them all
Glad to make your presence
Though I'm sure you're not excited

So strap in tight
You're going for a ride
Best of luck to you
You'll need it all to survive

## Roller Coaster of Grief

The news comes
Sometimes expected
Other times pure shock
From the trauma of it all

Your heart is racing
You feel sick
A million thoughts
race through your head

You are now strapped in
For the ride of your life
The ride that will never end
Only one way to get off

Tick tick tick you hear
Your being pulled uphill
The weight and pressure
So heavy on your chest

How did this happen
Why did this happen
You scream out in anger
The tears flow like a leaky faucet

Suddenly you're at the top
All is quiet for a moment in time
Your body is protecting you
Peace for mere seconds

You breathe in and out
But it doesn't last long
Soon you are plummeting
Down the steep hill

Now you can't catch your breath
You are frightened and confused
Where am I, you scream
I can't see anything

Objects go zooming past you
No chance to make them out
You go into a loop
All of a sudden you feel nothing

You're numb and the
Feeling is so strange
How do I explain this
It's scary and nice all the same

Instantly you are out of it
The crushing weight

It finds you again and
Wraps you up like a hug

Left and right you go
You don't have time to stop
Suddenly someone touches you
You look over

You aren't alone
There are others here too
The ride continues but you
Feel comforted for a moment

Though the roller coaster is
Unending and confusing
The fact is you are alive
And others surround you

Take a deep breath
Cry when needed
Scream and pound your fists
It's ok, everyone gets it

You are loved and safe
Be who you need to be
Welcome each of you
To the Rollercoaster of Grief

**You Matter**
In the Valleys of life
In the Mountains of life
It all matters
Because you matter

From a score at the buzzer
To a big sale on the job
To a graduation
To a wedding

To the missed field goal
To the promotion that you missed
To the job that was lost
To a relationship failed

All of it matters
Every bit of it matters
The big to the small
It matters because you matter

So when it comes to
The loss of someone
How can this ever be different
It's not

Everyone is wired different
Everyone deals with life
In their own unique ways
And it's perfectly ok

So if you find yourself
On a really bad day
Just know that it's ok
Because you matter

It doesn't matter that
No one else is feeling

What you are feeling
You matter so it matters

If a memory comes
Swooping in
And the tears fall
Like rain on a window

Tracing lines down your face
It's ok who sees
Because you matter
So it matters

If you feel joy one minute
And sadness the next
It's really ok
Because you matter

Don't compare or contrast
Your problems are real
You don't have to justify
What you are feeling at all

You matter
That's all that matters
We see you
You matter
The Truth

The Truth is it took
All the Strength
That I had to stand
Up and give your eulogy

I thought on the Adventures
That you went on
During your time in the military
And boy did you have a lot

The tour around Europe
On the boat that you
Had hanging in your room
Made by our grandfather

Your adventures while down
In New Orleans
And the amazing friends
That you made while down there

The friends that you made in
Florida and Michigan as well
Countless hours you had
Of stories to always share

I thought of our adventures together
The few balloon activities
That we shared in
Little Brother teaching you something

My flight with my pilot
The morning after you passed
As we soared into the sky
And I whispered through tears my goodbye

The strength to write my own poem
And share my gift with you

Just one last time
Art in words at its best

The strength to battle through
The excruciating pain of losing
You at such a young age
And knowing the loss was different

It wasn't going to go away
Like a blink of the eye
No sir, this would last
For a time unknown to me

The truth is
Some days really suck
And the grief can take over
At any second of the day

Flashes of anger and loneliness
Acceptance and denial
Jealousy of those who
Still have their siblings

It's an ugly truth
To this crazy adventure
Without you here with us
Gone for now but not forgotten

I find myself looking to the sky
Hoping to see your face
But I never do
But I know you're right there

Be it through a text message from
A friend asking how are you doing
Or in the cardinals I saw today
In the quiet of a moment

You are always right here
No matter where I go
So you want the truth
I love you always and forever

 Dan Older works as a professional transportation provider for people with nonmedical needs. In this capacity, he ushers people to and from their appointments with compassion and grace. In his down time, he is part of a hot-air balloon crew and enjoys the unique hobby of ghost hunting with his wife and friends.

In 2019, Dan's life changed when his only brother, Brad, died from a massive heart attack. Dan immediately started writing poetry to help process his thoughts and joined a support community that helped him see he wasn't alone.

Five years into his healing journey, he now leads a "Write Your Soul" meeting that encourages others to express themselves through writing. In addition to leading the group, he speaks at grief-oriented conferences and shares his poetry to help those who are hurting from a loss.

Dan lives in Michigan with his wife, Starr, and their fur baby, Ash.

Contact: danny_older@yahoo.com

# MY DEAD HUSBAND DIRECTED MY DATING LIFE

By Charity Hyams

I sat in the Skyline Chili in Newport Kentucky, with Ollie, my new love interest, next to me in the booth. After our first date the evening before, I'd stayed at his house instead of driving home. Instead of immediately parting ways, we decided to eat first. This was back in 2004, so to be honest, I don't remember the specifics of our conversation, but I do remember that it felt real in a way I had not experienced before.

I was going through my purse (the reason has been lost to the folds of time), and pulled out a little pewter heart about the size of a dime, you know, the kind of little charm you'd buy at the Hallmark store while checking out. My ADD squirrel brain loved stuff like that. In a rush of hopefulness or maybe connection, I'm not sure, I handed it to him. He took it, and for the next fifteen years it stayed tucked in his wallet.

Ollie was my best friend. Just by being in the same room, Ollie would have you laughing so hard that you were afraid you might never be able to stand up straight again. He would just take care of people, before they even asked. If someone's computer was broken, he would just fix it. He showed his love. We really did not like to be apart. His family called us Ollity. If we were not at work, we were together. We married, moved around the country, and had three beautiful boys whom Ollie absolutely adored.

In 2018, our minivan fell on Ollie while he was underneath it fixing a belt. I was standing above the van and he told me to pull the lever on the belt. If there was any time in my life where I wish I had not listened to one of his requests, it would be that one. When I pulled the lever the faulty jack tipped, and the car fell on his chest. I called 911 while I mad scrambled to get the jack cranked back down and then back up again in time to save his life. Eventually (maybe seven to fifteen minutes later), two police officers arrived on the scene and we extricated him from under the vehicle. He was still breathing at that point, but they sent me away to gather my keys and get my purse while he was loaded into the ambulance. When the ambulance didn't immediately move away, sirens screaming, I knew.

When I arrived at the hospital, they put me in the little room. Anyone who has been in the little room knows what that means. It means nothing good. I looked at my friend, Laura, who had come with me, and said, "He's dead." She said, "It might not mean that." But I knew. I knew before they told me. Before I even stepped into that room.

That day, after I retrieved Ollie's wallet, I took the little heart out of its pocket—the heart that had made a heart-shaped impression in the worn leather, the heart that had lived in Ollie's pocket for fifteen years—and placed it in my own wallet, tucking it safely into the corner of a zippered pocket. Many times over the coming months, I found myself reaching into that recessed pocket just to touch it. It was a little metal piece of reassurance—proof of a love that once was and in my heart always would be.

Seven months later, I decided to dip my toe into the dating world. (I had tried around six months, but I was not ready and it was a mess. You can read about that in *The Widow's Guide to Dating*

132

if you really want to). This time, I connected with a man who was going through a really ugly divorce. We connected on a level that was more than a just a hook up, but things just seemed too complicated for a relationship, so we were discussing a friend with benefits setup. He didn't think that was going to work for him either, so we were having a "breakup" talk. (Although I have to wonder: is it a breakup if it isn't even a relationship yet? Anyway.) We had both sat silently on the couch for a few minutes when suddenly Amazon's Alexa chimed in with, "Here's a song I think you will enjoy," and played "Blame it on Me" by George Ezra. In the chorus, the singer tells the listener to blame them for any bad things that are happening.

I felt that Ollie was just saying look, if you have no better reason to just end it, just blame it on me, do it now. No use dragging it out. I looked over at this man and said, "That's my dead husband," and burst out laughing until I cried.

So many times throughout my first year, especially on birthdays, anniversaries, and bad days, I would turn on the music and certain songs would play that felt like Ollie was sending them. One of them was "Thinking Out Loud" by Ed Sheeran. In the first stanza, he muses about his love's legs not working any more and whether she'll still remember that he loves her.

When Ollie was under the van, I first tried to lift it off of him by myself. Then I helped lift it with a police officer, but the van fell again and we had to lift the van a second time. After that day, I lost all feeling in my right pinky toe, ring toe, middle toe, and on the right side of my foot. I had scans and tried physical therapy, chiropractic care, epidural steroidal injections, acupuncture, massage—anything to release the blocked nerves and relieve the symptoms. (As an interesting sidenote, in Eastern medicine the yang [male] energy rules the right side of the body, so I always thought it was interesting that my right foot "died" at the same time as Ollie.) No matter what I did, my foot remained the same. It was an external reminder of a huge internal loss.

Dating after loss is hard, and so I would date for a month and take a break. Rinse and repeat that cycle. After not dating for a good three months and then starting again (although it leaned more toward hook ups because, let's be honest, dating can be brutal), I met Franz. We had consensual sex twice, two days in a row, and then he left to go back to Peru. We spent a month together the next summer and once again parted ways, fully expecting to never see each other again. And in the way of relationships that have no future, we stopped talking because talking sometimes hurts.

In October of that year, while getting a massage to fix a slipped disk in my spinal column, my back finished the process and herniated completely. I lost all control of my right foot and began walking in a style that my child's nanny at the time referred to as "zombi-ing it." Picture Michael Jackson's "Thriller" video. I had to make the hard choice of having a risky surgery as a solo parent, which meant making sure my will was ready and having everything in play in case the worst happened. I impulsively texted Franz and said, "I'm going into surgery. If anything happens, we're good and I love you." Ok, it was actually a little more than that, but I don't remember exactly what I wrote anymore and it really doesn't matter for this story. He texted back; he was in New York City. We started talking again after my surgery.

From November to December, I had one nanny leave to take a corporate position and our second nanny had to return home because her long-term boyfriend had gotten into a horrible accident and was in a full body cast. During this time, I was limited on how much weight I could pick up and how much I could move around. Franz and I spoke a lot and on a much more serious level. We decided to make a go of it, but I still had doubts. I had many moments where I directly questioned the universe, asking whether I should move ahead with Franz or not.

I received my answer the day I took Arantza to the airport to catch her flight home. She felt horrible for leaving, especially since I still needed help, but we both knew she needed to be back home. I encouraged her to go and to not feel guilty. I knew I would need to see my boyfriend with my own eyes after a horrible accident. At the same time, I also knew that Franz had canceled his ticket home to Peru and was going to come to Vermont in the next couple of days. I was scared. Summoning up my focus once again, I thought, *Ollie, if this is the right thing, I need a CLEAR sign. Like direct, buddy. I love you so much.*

As a widow with children, serious relationships are nothing to mess around with. Yes, I could get hurt again, but that I could deal with. That I could work through. But I did not want to mess up my kids anymore. That I could not bear.

What if Franz came and they hated him? What if they loved him and he left us? What if he abused them? What if he treated them like stepchildren? What if he was just indifferent?

I realized I knew what to do in all of these horrible scenarios, but even the thought of putting my babies through more trauma after all they already endured made me sick to my stomach.

After dropping Arantza off and hugging her goodbye, I got back in the car and turned on the ignition. The radio came to life and "Thinking Out Loud" by Ed Sheeran started playing. "You gotta do better than that this time," I said out loud to Ollie. I started the two hour drive home thinking about all the arrangements that had to be made—not only for Franz moving in, but also for Christmas and my youngest's third birthday. Mentally, I started running through schedules, physical therapy appointments, and general life to-dos.

But I had asked Ollie for a clearer sign. When I got home, I put my purse on the table and it fell to the side. My wallet fell out and the heart *plinked* onto the table. My heart. Ollie's heart. The heart I'd given Ollie on our first date, that had lived in his wallet, that now lived in mine. The heart that had been tucked away in the corner of a still-closed zippered pocket. I looked up and said, "Thank you, my Love."

Franz and I are married now. We made our family of five a family of six with the addition of our daughter. The boys love him and call him Papa. Ollie is Daddo (even to Franz and my daughter). Five years later Franz and I are going strong. We both feel Ollie's presence and when we get signs we both go, "That's Ollie!" There is no need for Ollie to direct my dating life anymore, but he still makes his presence known especially when we need it.

I still ask for help. I still ask for signs. Just last week I lost an important document that I thought we needed for a meeting the next day. I didn't find the document, but I found the heart and I knew deep down it all was going to be ok. "Thank you, my Love."

In the early days of loss, we can feel like we are living in a cloud of grief. We might not feel at all connected to our person who is on the other side, and that is ok. Know that this is perfectly normal. When I was going through that time, I used my reminders of Ollie a lot. I often reached for my heart in my wallet, for his wedding ring that I wore around my neck, his shirt I kept in a plastic bag so I could keep his smell as long as I could. I used my reminders to maintain my connection to him and comfort myself. Use the reminders that were left here for you until that fog lifts.

I also want to remind you that if you feel like you experience a sign, give it to yourself. In the full context of life and the universe, do I 100 percent know the mechanics and can I absolutely guarantee the authenticity of everything I have felt has been a sign? Nope. Does it matter to me even a little bit? Nope.

Why? Because it makes me feel better. It makes me feel connected to someone I love, and I feel like if he could send me a sign, he would. So I accept the little happenstances that feel like signs because they HELP me, and isn't that the point? You notice what gets you through the day. You give yourself what puts a smile on your face and makes you feel loved. Go on and try it. I won't tell anyone and you don't have to either.

 Charity Pimentel-Hyams is a widow, healer, wife, day-trader, stay-at-home mother, speaker, coach, and author. Her two books, *The Widow's Survival Guide Living with Children After the Death of Your Spouse* and *The Widow's Guide to Dating Sex, Love, and Relationships after the Death of Your Spouse* were Amazon bestsellers. She is currently working on her third book to help the helpers of grief. She holds a bachelor of science and many certifications in the healing arts. She resides in rural Vermont in an 1840s farmhouse with her alive husband Franz and her four school-aged children. Her interest in the healing arts, writing, and coaching has led to a career in public speaking and writing, where she helps light the way for healing and wholeness and finding joy in the midst of grief and chaos. You can connect with Charity on Instagram or tiktok at @ livingonbycharity .

# GRIEF IS HARD WORK

By Nora Rose

Have you ever curled up under the covers and cried because the loss of your person was too much to think about? Have you ever felt like you couldn't get out of bed because of the intense sadness? Have you wondered, *Is this real?*

Unfortunately, it *is* real. They really are gone! You will never hear their voice again, and suddenly you have so much to ask them. There will never be another phone call, hug, or "I love you." After that, depression sets in and your world stops, yet the outside world keeps going. Family members, friends, and neighbors go about their business like nothing has changed except for you! But for you, everything has changed and it may never be the same. Who will understand this? NOBODY!

When my mom died in January 2014, a piece of my heart was ripped out of me along with my identity, and I experienced this surreal state of being. She passed away on one of the coldest days of winter, when the windchill was forty degrees below zero. Everything was frozen, including my heart. When I got home after my mother's wake, I discovered the furnace had gone out and the bathroom pipes had frozen and burst. There were shards of ice all over the garage floor. It was an apt metaphor for how I felt—shattered and scattered about.

Was I still a daughter? I am half her and her DNA flows through my veins. I try hard to remember that nothing can take that away from me, and it gives my broken heart a little comfort. I was lucky to have a mom who loved me unconditionally and encouraged me like she did. I miss our relationship.

Laying under the covers with my eyes closed, memories from my childhood flash through my mind. Thinking back, I realize my mom endured all the pain when my dad died and made it easier for my sister and me. I feel now what she may have gone through then. My sister and I were so young and she was so strong for us.

When you're grieving, friends and family will tell you your loved one is in a better place. They will say things like, "They are not suffering anymore," and, "You took such good care of her." Weeks later, they'll ask, "Why are you still crying?"

I don't know. In this state, useless thoughts come up like, *Did I make the right medical decisions? I wanted her to die at home in her own bed. I didn't bring the right underwear to the funeral home.* I am so relieved that the dress she wanted to wear for her wake, the one she wore to my wedding, is hanging in the closet. I am so grateful she purchased her burial plot years ago when my father died. There are so many decisions! I've helped manage her business and did her taxes for years, but now I have to do it myself. She made this easier for me and yet it's still so difficult. Why does everything feel different? What's wrong with my thinking? I'm a grown woman, but I feel like a child. She prepared me for this day, but I just want to scream, *I'M NOT READY!* I am at a loss and in complete despair. My world as I know it is no longer.

My children were the external force pushing me forward. It took a long time, but finally my internal drive felt ready to take on the work of rebuilding my life. I listened to music to soothe myself. I meditated in bed with recorded guidance from Oprah and Deepak Chopra, sometimes three times a day, because it calmed me. I found an online writing program for grief. I grabbed my pen and notebook and wrote my heart out, then shared with the group. I googled "grief" to see if what I felt was normal because no one talks about grief. I had to search for information. When I broke down crying in my doctor's office, he said I was depressed and I needed to do something fun. After watching a video about Jack Canfield, who created the *Chicken Soup for the Soul* series and offers life coaching programs, I made some phone calls to ask how to enroll. in his events. Surely, if other people had overcome their traumas by participating in the programs, then I could too? I signed up for his Train the Trainer program, which was a year-long commitment.

The first conference was in Long Beach, California and lasted a week. As I checked in at registration, they asked me simple questions about where I was from and why I was there, and I burst into tears. I was alone, immersed in a very large crowd and overwhelmed that complete strangers had asked me these questions as soon as I arrived. They sent my fragile self to a volunteer named Forrest and I revealed my grief. He had a calm, kind voice and an incredible brain injury accident and recovery. We are still friends today. As the week wore on, I met new, inspirational people to talk with, heart hug, meditate, visualize, and learn Canfield's success principles. We did small group activities and exchanged more stories. It comforted me to become friends with two young women who had also lost their moms. We gravitated toward each other. Some participants said they hadn't talked to their mothers in months. REALLY?! If they only understood how I would cherish one more conversation with my mom. I reminded them how they are missing a wonderful opportunity to find out more about their mom's childhood, work experience, and her dreams. What did you do for her birthday? I encouraged them to call their moms and ask if she'd had a good day. I reminded my fellow attendees that even if their childhoods hadn't gone the way they wanted, their moms had done the best they could. One person instantly sent a text to her mom, while others said they would call their moms soon! Another participant said he hated his parents because of his childhood. What?! I told him maybe one day he could forgive them. Interacting with his energy was difficult for me.

By the third evening I was exhausted and I reflected on all the experiences I encountered. I realized the relationship with my mom and dad was not the same kind of relationship other participants had with their parents. Everyone was at this conference for different reasons: abuse, addiction, betrayal, business failures/ideas, chronic illness, divorce, and trauma. They all wanted a better way to cope, to overcome their obstacles, and think better.

Over the course of the training, we all read Jack Canfield's book, *The Success Principles*. In the book, it said your mess is your message and you should lean into it. So I leaned into learning. I had to find a purpose for my pain—my mess. Everyone in the room had suffered or had a hardship or a setback at some point in their lives, and we were all in it together, giving what we could and taking what we needed. We helped each other.

I shared from my heart and set new goals. I left this first training with work to do. My goal was to write a children's book. I also had to teach the success principles to a group of people. How was I going to do that?

One of my daughters was back from college, so I asked her if a few of her friends would want me to coach them. So, once a month from February until June, Lauren, Allissa, and Jocelyn came over and sat in my living room to talk, do activities, make vision boards, and set goals. They wanted to do a culminating activity at the end. We discussed several ideas and I told them they could decide what to do. Guess what they picked? Skydiving! We decided to jump out of an airplane in June. My new purpose kept me busy. I did research on publishing a book and skydiving. I even taught a meditation class at the local high school.

My dad's birthday was upon us, so my daughters and I went to a Cubs' game then got a cake to celebrate his memory. He loved baseball and had played in the Navy. I also hung a photo of my mom in the kitchen so I could say "Hello" or "I'm sorry" to her. As her care-taker and power of attorney when she was alive, I still felt guilty for making major decisions about her health, especially when she didn't get the results we were told she would after a medical procedure.

Finally, it was June! Skydiving was an amazing, adrenaline-filled experience where your senses come alive. I said a quick prayer on the plane ride up to 15,000 feet and wondered whether Mom was with me as I looked out the window to a clear sunny day. In the plane, twelve of us sat on a bench, and scooted forward when it was our turn to jump. I was attached to an expert skydiver instructor with bands under my arms and around my thighs. I was doing a tandem skydive, where the expert takes charge of all the vital functions, such as opening the parachute and landing safely. Each person jumped out a few seconds apart, along with a cameraman. When it was my turn, my jump partner and I counted to three before cartwheeling out of the airplane into a fast, ferociously windy, sixty-second upside-down free fall through blurry white clouds and cold air. I was immersed with the elements of the sky in just a T-shirt and leggings. It was like a jump into freedom!

When the instructor pulled open the first parachute, we quickly flew back up in the air and turned right-side up before starting to fall again. The cameraman was right there with us taking photos and video. We shifted our bodies to a flying position with our arms out and knees bent. The camera guy gave hand signals to the instructor. I made a heart shape in the air, then gave him a thumbs up and a wave as the instructor and I glided in the sky. When the cameraman drifted away the instructor pulled open the big parachute. We began to float upward again, but when I looked down I saw land. It was the same view you see out of an airplane during takeoff or landing. As we floated over a highway the instructor pulled on the thick heavy ropes of the parachute to turn us around and send us in the direction we wanted to go. If he said lean, I leaned. We drifted toward a grassy area where he told me how to land. Once we were all on the ground,

I found my group and we hugged with giddy excitement. Our family members, who had watched our dives, celebrated with us. It is a moment we still talk about today.

Shortly after that, I visited a psychic on a whim, to see if there was a message from my mom. The psychic looked at me and said there was someone swearing and waving their arms in the air, saying, "Are you crazy?!" The psychic asked what I'd done. I smiled and knew Mom was with me. She was out of control because I went skydiving!

At my next Train the Trainer week with Team Canfield, I was excited to high-five and hug all the familiar faces. We were divided into groups to share our homework and given a success principle to teach on stage to hundreds of attendees who were the audience. We each had separate speaking parts, and when it was my turn, I walked to the edge of the stage, put my arms out, and said, "I cartwheeled out of an airplane at 15,000 feet and THREW MYSELF BACK INTO LIFE!" The projector screen behind me displayed photos of my experience. Some audience members cheered!

When I hugged people after the week was over, some didn't want to let go. Others said they felt my mother's presence (her love) through me. One group of students even went skydiving afterward! I graduated from the Train the Trainer program with many new friends. The love and connection I found there helped mend my broken heart. I inspired people by being my authentic self, tears and all. I even went back to assist on Team Canfield to refresh myself on the principles and to help others also learn to help themselves.

Throughout my grief experience, I wondered, "Who can help me?" The answer is: I can help me. You can help yourself. We can grieve and honor our loved ones in our own special way. We can live with grief and joy simultaneously when we express ourselves and know their love is always with us.

Whether you've lost a home, a job, or a loved one, the experience creates an emotional wound that requires us to heal. Everyone will have their own unique grief experience at some point in their lives.

There's no escaping it. Your version of normalcy changes beyond your control, and the truth is, especially in today's world, that version of normal may not return quickly. So be patient with yourself and others, and show empathy. Start with a simple plan and take baby steps to move forward. Choose what's best for you. Join that class. Attend that club. Connect with people who will listen and help you. Communicate what you need. I encourage you to talk about your grief, share your story, and surround yourself with people who lift you up!

It's not easy. It takes work. It doesn't get better in a day, a week or a month, and sometimes not even in a year. However, as you practice what you like, whether that is writing, meditation, yoga, tennis, working out, or something else, you will gradually start to see results. New experiences and new people will enter your life to fill the void. You will lift yourself up and find yourself again.

Nora Rose is a middle school teacher, coach, speaker, and recipient of the Parent and Teacher Choice Award for her books *Gabriel's Journey, A Journal, a Recipe, and a Family in America*, and *Bentley's Week*. She has coauthored several books, including the #1 best-selling book *Goodness Abounds: 365 True Stories of Loving Kindness*. She holds a Bachelor of Arts in Education, a Master of Arts in Curriculum and Instruction, and a Master of Arts in Health Communication from Marquette University. When Nora is not writing, she enjoys reading books, water sports, swimming, scuba diving, kayaking, playing with her dog, and traveling the world with her family.

# FLOODED WITH TEARS

*By Leslie Rott and Molly Cohen*

Augthat 11, 2014, was Leslie's twenty-ninth Birthday. The last text Leslie received from our dad was that morning, wishing her a happy birthday. The last text she sent him, not knowing it would be the last, was, "Thank you! Love you too!" And that was it. The message was just five words, two of which may be the most important in the English language. But Leslie feels she took them for granted, not knowing at the time that they were the last five words she would ever send to our dad.

The last interaction Molly had with our dad was the night prior, and she will regret the encounter (or the lack thereof) for the rest of her life. She was caught in that foggy stage of sleep where she could hear everything but couldn't wake up unless it was to an alarm. She heard his quiet steps entering her room and then the warmth of fresh laundry that he set on her bed. She could have said "Goodnight," but she didn't because she figured she would see him again. She did, but he was lying in a coffin. Deep down, she knows that he felt loved, but she will forever regret not waking up for him.

Regret. Hindsight is 20/20. Looking backward is a funny thing. We are both filled with regret, not knowing that the interactions we had with our dad at the time, as meaningless as they may have seemed, held, and still hold, so much meaning. There were things we would have done differently if we would have known. But if we had known, we also never would have let him walk out the door that day. We would have held him tight and protected our dad from the storm that none of us knew was coming.

When Leslie returned home to her apartment in New York after celebrating her birthday, she noticed Facebook posts about flooding in Michigan. She reached out to our mom to make sure everything was okay, only to find out that our dad had never made it home from work. Our mom attempted to report our dad missing, but every local police department refused to take a report because it hadn't been 24–48 hours. Our dad was never even fifteen minutes late, and he wasn't answering his phone, so this was completely out of character for him.

Leslie spent the next day—August 12—walking around like a zombie. She couldn't concentrate on work, knowing that our dad was missing. Surrounded by millions of people in New York, she'd never felt more alone and more isolated. She texted her friend, who was a police officer, to find out what more she should do. She also texted a friend whose best friend had gone missing. Neither of them had easy answers.

Molly also reached out to those she knew and who she hoped could help. But in the end, it was to no avail. After looking for our dad and going to the police, Molly and our mom came home to an empty house, with no father or husband in sight. Silence. The next few hours that followed were a whirlwind of emotions. Molly and our mom went from silence to talking about our dad, to discussing what he could possibly be doing if he was not home.

Then, at 8:30 p.m., our world changed forever. That moment will forever be burned into Molly's brain. The silence was interrupted by a knock at the door and for one millisecond, Molly and our mom had hope. Hope that was diminished by a police officer who handed our mom a crumpled piece of paper and said, "Ma'am, you should call this number immediately." Our mom pleaded with him to tell her what was going on, but all he did was reiterate that she needed to call the number on the piece of paper. Our mom called, as always, leaving the phone on speaker, so Molly heard ringing and then another "Ma'am…" This time, the man's voice was ominous. The officer on the other line told our mom that he was a detective from Hazel Park who had found our dad in his car. Dead.

As she heard the news, Molly's knees gave out and for the next five minutes, all she could do was scream. He was gone, and we were going to have to figure out how to live life without our father. Our mom politely responded to the detective with "Thank you, I have to hang up to take care of my daughter." Molly is forever indebted to our mom, who proceeded to hug her. Molly still feels guilty that our mom was strong for her at a time where she should have been grieving as well.

We'd like to believe that the situation would have turned out differently if law enforcement had started looking for him immediately. But he was not found by the police. He was found by someone living on the street where he'd ended up. The police are supposed to serve and protect, but on that night, they did neither. We suffered for over twenty-four hours waiting to hear news about our dad, and ultimately, the news we received was not what we were hoping for.

Leslie does not remember the drive to the airport or the flight to Michigan. She does remember hugging Molly the hardest she ever had when she finally got out of the airport. She remembers sitting with Molly in the backseat of Molly's friend's car. She remembers Molly's friend ripping off pieces of bagel and trying to get Molly to eat something. She remembers being struck by the fact that she did not realize people that age had that capacity for such kindness and compassion. It was such a simple gesture, and yet so profound in a moment where nothing in the world made sense.

She also remembers seeing our dad in his casket, an image that will never be erased from her mind. She remembers thinking that he looked like himself, but not. She doesn't remember how she held it together, but she thinks she barely did. She couldn't breathe, couldn't think. The heart takes much longer to process what the mind already knows.

Our dad grew up collecting butterflies, and in the limo on the way to the cemetery, all of a sudden there was a butterfly flying around inside. There were other butterfly sightings throughout the day and in the days that followed. People told us that butterflies flew around them or landed on them, and they felt like our dad was with them.

After the funeral, we heard similar stories of people seeing signs of our dad. During the funeral, the Rabbi told a story about our dad making Molly a Goldfish cracker box costume for Halloween. Someone told us afterward that they had looked under the pew in front of them, and there was a Goldfish Cracker lying on the floor. What are the chances of finding a Goldfish cracker in a funeral home? It's not really a place for kids, is it?

When Leslie returned to New York, a question she commonly got was, "Was your dad sick for long?" It was incredibly frustrating. Not everyone who dies is sick. Would a protracted illness have been preferable to an unexpected and unforeseen event? No one can say for sure. We certainly can't. To us, losing our dad the way we did was unfathomable, and nearly ten years later it still haunts both of us.

The flooding that occurred in Michigan on August 11, 2014, turned out to be the second-heaviest day of rainfall in the state's history, with 4.37 inches of rainfall, three inches of which fell between 5:00 p.m. and 8:00 p.m. The only day in recorded history with greater rainfall was in July 1925, when 4.74 inches fell. Some people have suggested that we won't see another rainfall and flooding in Michigan like we did on August 11, 2014, for at least another 100 years, but potentially 500 years. The average rainfall for the entire month of August is three inches. For us, our world is forever changed. A rainstorm will never just be a rainstorm again. An unanswered cell phone call or text message will always cause fear and trepidation that something bad has happened.

While some of the motorists who were stranded on the road were rescued by emergency personnel, our dad died alone in his car, parked on a residential street. As our mom says, our dad was never alone. We are a family that prides itself on our togetherness. So why, on this particular night, was he alone? Why couldn't he have made it home to be with his family? Why did he have to stop on some random residential street, which ultimately would be the place where he took his last breath?

For us, this was our Hurricane Katrina. As we drove through neighborhood after affected neighborhood, the scene became even more troubling. The contents of peoples' lives were strewn across their front lawns. But despite the carnage, we lost so much more. We still get chills when we look at photographs from the flood. It's surreal. It's so unbelievable that it happened at all, let alone the fact that we lost our dad as a result. To this day, we cannot look at pictures of the flood and its aftermath without feeling sick to our stomachs.

August 11 will always remain Leslie's birthday. How does she live with that? How does she celebrate the day of her birth while simultaneously mourning the loss of our father? Maybe it's just a lesson in life. Life comes with good and bad. Sometimes good and bad things happen at the same time; sometimes they happen at different times. And sometimes we have no control over what happens when. We were robbed of the chance of having our dad watch us graduate from college and graduate school, of our dad walking us down the aisle and dancing with us at our weddings, and of the chance to have him be a grandfather to our children. While many lost possessions in the flood, we lost something so much more precious.

In order to cope with the loss of our father, Leslie turned to advocacy and Molly turned to religion. Leslie tried to get a law passed that would prevent police departments in Michigan from refusing to take missing persons reports even if it has been less than twenty-four hours. While our dad joined the ranks of the missing, he also joined the ranks of the found. So many are not. And their families have to live with not knowing what happened for the rest of their lives.

So while we have that peace, we also have regret. Regret that we didn't post on social media that our dad was missing. Regret that Find My Phone didn't exist back then and we couldn't have easily located our dad without the help (or lack thereof) of the police. But with that regret also comes the knowledge and understanding that we can still make a difference. That by telling our story, we can help others who have been and may go through, something similar.

When our dad died, it was personal. We mourned for ourselves, and we mourned for anyone else who has had to experience the pain of having a family member go missing. We lamented that the police did a woefully poor job in handling the situation. And we wanted closure.

Our story is personal, but it is also about so much more than us. We lost things in the flood that will never be replaced. We also learned, unfortunately, that "the bad cop" is an all too common trope. And we learned that those who are paid to serve and protect fail and are not called to account for their failure. But we've also learned that there are good, compassionate people in the world.

We worry that one day we'll wake up and won't be able to remember our dad's face or the sound of his voice. We're worried that one day all that will be left is a blank space that can never be filled. Closure will likely never come in the form of explanations or understanding or apologies. It will not come from police officers or politicians, people in power who have the power to make a difference. It will only come if we allow it. If we let it in. If we let the past be the past and focus on the future. But a future without our dad sometimes seems unimaginable.

Leslie was 29 when our dad died. Molly was 19. Our dad was 63. And as it turns out, our dad was only a seven-minute drive away from home, a cruel irony considering the closeness yet helpless distance we felt. These ages mark profound moments in our lives. Leslie was just settling into her career, and Molly was on the brink of adulthood still finding her path. These numbers aren't just figures; they represent pivotal points in our lives, forever changed by his absence.

We don't know how we are supposed to feel being at the cemetery. Connected to our dad in some way? The place we can go to "see" and visit him? It feels like a bad consolation prize for not having him physically around. It's hard to imagine life moving forward without our dad, but it has to. We don't have a choice, or we die too. Sometimes we want to scream, shouting to everyone within earshot that our dad died, as if that explained everything, as if that was all they needed to know about us.

Molly has a favorite poem, "The Dash" by Linda Ellis, that she read at our father's funeral. When it comes to death, we can look at it two ways. We can look at it as the date of birth and the date of death, of coming into the world alone and leaving it alone, or we can look at everything in the finite but wonderful space between those two dates, and be grateful for the time we had with our dad, even though it was not and never will be long enough.

Although we wrote this chapter together, we wanted to provide you with individual messages about coping with loss. Grief transcends time and this is what it looks like for us, ten years later.

Leslie: If you are new to grieving, know this—life goes on but your grief does not go away. You grow with it. You grow into it. You grow around it. You learn to breathe and function again, if not for yourself, at first, for your loved ones. You do this because at the end of the day, the person you lost would want you to continue to live even though they are no longer alive. Surround yourself with people who will support you and love you through your grief, who will allow you to share memories and not force you to forget. All of our experiences, good and bad, make us who we are. This is a part of you, but it does not define you.

Molly: Overcoming loss is a journey marked by moments of profound sorrow and gradual acceptance. While time may soften the sharp edges of grief, the ache of missing someone or something remains a constant companion in everyday life. Yet, in navigating this emotional landscape, there's a resilience that emerges, a testament to the enduring love and memories shared. Grief becomes a familiar presence that is embraced and a clear sign that past love keeps you moving forward in the darkest times. You're changed, and different, but still moving forward.

*Leslie Rott*

Leslie Rott has a master's degree and a PhD in sociology from the University of Michigan, and a master's degree in health advocacy from Sarah Lawrence College. She was diagnosed with lupus and rheumatoid arthritis in 2008, at the age of 22. She is a blogger, e-patient, health activist, patient advocate, healthcare disruptor, sociologist, and writer. She authors the blog *Getting Closer to Myself* (www.gettingclosertomyself.blogspot.com) and has contributed to a variety of other health-related sites, including CreakyJoints, Health Central, Health Line, Lupus News Today, Mango Health, and Rheumatoidarthritis.net. Leslie's story has been featured in the U.S. Pain Foundation Invisible Project: RA/RD Edition, *Women's Health* magazine (twice!), *Real Life Diaries: Living with Rheumatic Diseases*, and on a jacket, "Double Major," that she proudly wears as a member of the Walking Gallery of Healthcare. She currently works as the Compliance & Experience Officer at a community healthcare company in Royal Oak, Michigan. Leslie lives in Beverly Hills, Michigan, with her son and husband.

*Molly Cohen*

Molly Cohen is a graduate student at Sara Schenirer/Yeshiva University's Wurzweiler School of Social Work. She received her bachelor of arts in Spanish with a minor in biology from Wayne State University. She is passionate about perinatal and maternal mental health and helping others through some of life's most difficult moments. Although she is unsure of her future career, she is grateful for the opportunity to find her path through social work. She interned at Jewish Family Service of Metro Detroit and is currently interning at a Perinatal and Youth mental health clinic. Molly lives in Southfield, Michigan, with her husband and daughter.

*Neal Barry Rott*
*December 17, 1951–August 12, 2014*

# EMBRACING LOSS: A JOURNEY TO HEALING AND RENEWAL

*By Laura E Summers*

I was plunged into grief before I even reached puberty. My dad was too young to die in an airplane crash. As I began to process the unfathomable news, questions flooded my mind. *Who would guide me through my teenage years? Who would help me choose which college to attend? Who would walk beside me down the aisle on my wedding day? Who would I be if I wasn't Daddy's girl?*

These moments in time, out of our control, reshape our destinies. Grief changes us. As I faced my uncertain future, I couldn't imagine who I would become. What lay ahead? And, amidst all this turmoil, would I ever recognize the girl in the mirror again?

Grieving is hard—it sucks, actually. Yes, this multifaceted beast is a natural response to loss. But, each time it happens, it's a whole new experience. If, like me, you've lost more than one person, you may notice that grieving for a second person may feel different. For example, one of my clients (I'll call her Ella), unexpectedly lost her son. Grief took a tight hold, and she and her husband clung to one another in the depths of their darkness. Then, her husband lost a long, arduous battle with cancer. Ella asked me why she didn't feel the same anguish for her husband that she did for their son. Although she was overwhelmed with sadness both times, the pain felt different. The love we hold for our children differs from the love we share with our spouse. Each bond is unique, singular, and incomparable. So it's only natural to process the grief from their losses differently as well.

Sorrow touches us in many ways. For instance, when a relationship ends, we retire, or our pet passes away. Losing a job we loved, having financial struggles, or going through a big accident are also sources of unhappiness. Grieving can happen after a miscarriage, a betrayal, or an intense scare. Even happy times, like our kids starting kindergarten or going to college, may make us feel sad. We grieve when our health changes or when someone we care about gets sick. Grief can come when a special dream doesn't come true, when we move away from our home or friends, or when a parent gets remarried and we become a stepchild.

When my father died, I cried. Someone told me that as the oldest child, I should be strong and stop the tears. Yet, crying was essential to my healing journey. Their words inadvertently slowed my ability to process my agony. There are no rules in grief. What you are feeling is perfectly natural for what you are experiencing. The pain of loss can be overwhelming. Difficult and unexpected emotions can show up. From shock and anger to disbelief, guilt, and deep sadness, the depth of the emotions we feel can literally paralyze us. One of life's biggest challenges is learning to cope with the loss of someone you love. I'm glad you're here and reading this book because you don't have to walk the path of grief alone.

My parents were my first experiences with unconditional love and with deep grief. I was thirteen when my dad died. Flying was his passion, and he died doing something he loved. As a self-proclaimed daddy's girl, I jumped at every opportunity to join him in the plane. He gave me my own logbook for tracking the hours I flew as his copilot, and after each flight I proudly recorded our journey. I lost that book years ago, but I still remember its brown leather cover with my name embossed in gold letters at the bottom right.

My dad's death changed the course of my life. Grief made me angry. I was angry at him for leaving, angry at God for taking him, and angry at the world for continuing to go on. I felt guilt and responsibility, too. I convinced myself that if I had been with him in that plane, I could have landed it safely and saved his life.

I was fortunate to still have my mother. She was a beautiful soul with a bright smile. She cherished her daughters (I have three younger sisters), and she instilled in us the values of strength, independence, and resiliency. But two years after my father passed, she remarried. That marriage was another source of grief for me. My stepfather and I had an undeniable friction. Just over a year into their union, she confided to me that it wasn't working and she intended to file for divorce. Tragically, before she took any steps to do so, she had a brain aneurysm. A week later, as I stood by her hospital bed holding her hand, she died. I was sixteen. Once again, grief washed over me, leaving an indelible mark and catapulting my life in yet another new direction.

Even after loss, joy can touch our lives. After my mom died, I met a handsome young man and we fell in love. We were happy, and soon I learned I was pregnant. The news made me feel both excited and scared. It was a combination of emotions that I now refer to as *nerve-cited*. I was worried about the future. Without my mom around to guide me, how could I be a good mom? Tragically, I lost my precious baby boy, whom I named Eric. This grief felt different from losing my parents and it has remained a constant companion, lingering deep in my heart.

Lots of factors influence how grief affects us. Our personality and coping styles, as well as our age and life experiences, play significant roles. Our faith and belief system also greatly impacts how we process grief and what type of support resonates as comforting and appropriate.

In 1969, psychiatrist Elizabeth Kubler-Ross published the five stages of grief. I didn't experience all of them, but I became best friends with some.

Denial. Our reality shifts when we experience loss. Denial is the protective shield our minds put up to give us breathing room to process the emotion and information. When I lost my son, I sat in the warm sun on the windowsill of my hospital room, feeling over-whelming sadness and utter disbelief that my baby was gone. I was sure a nurse would walk into my room with him in her arms. But she never did.

Anger. Anger lingered with me for a while. I isolated myself and held the pain inside. Grief coaching loosened its grip. But the real game-changer was forgiveness. Forgiving my parents and my son for leaving me and forgiving God for taking them gave me the strength to let go. And it allowed me to honor their memories from a place of love. Anger isn't a great place to camp out in. It can bring about various negative consequences, including negative health impacts and a delayed grieving journey.

Bargaining. You might obsess over what you could have done differently. Or you might make promises to yourself or God like, "I promise to be better if [*fill in the blank*]." You might also replay moments in your mind when you wished you had said or done something different. This is where my guilt of not being with my dad kicked in. If only I had been there, I could have flown the plane and saved him. The truth is, had I been there, I likely would have died too.

Depression. When our thoughts begin to calm and we start to see the reality of our situation, we may feel depressed. Everything feels heavy and hard to bear. Depression can leave us feeling alone. If you're feeling depressed, I encourage you to reach out and ask for help. Find a support group, talk to a grief therapist, or connect with a life coach who specializes in grief healing. Remember that friend or family member who asked what they could do to help? Call them. Tell them you need to talk and would appreciate their willingness to listen.

Acceptance. Acceptance doesn't mean the pain and sadness magically disappears. I wish it did. But acceptance means we stop resisting the reality of our situation. It means facing the truth even when it's hard. Reaching this state means allowing ourselves to feel our sadness and our love sitting side by side. Acceptance is the beginning of healing. When we accept our present circumstances, it paves the way for us to move forward and explore new possibilities.

Some schools of thought include two more stages of grief: shock and testing. Shock may include a numbed feeling of disbelief at the news of a loss. The gift of shock is that it can aid in protecting us from a deep sense of overwhelm. Testing can present itself as searching for solutions to cope with loss.

It's important to know that your grief is uniquely yours. You may experience all seven stages of grief, five, three, or none. You may find, like me, that anger and bargaining happen at the same time. Or you may have worked through your depression, only to have it reemerge. Rest assured that what you are experiencing is exactly what you need right now.

So, how do we weather grief? First, it's important to be gentle and kind to yourself. Give yourself permission to feel without judging what comes up. Make sure to take care of your physical, emotional, and mental needs. Dealing with grief is a lot like recovering from a serious illness—some days will be tough, while others will be better. It's not a linear path. Knowing and respecting your personal boundaries and limits is beneficial. Also, letting others help you with tasks can give them a sense of purpose and lighten your load.

Remember that grief can make it hard to think clearly, leading to impulsive decisions that you might regret later. Big decisions like moving or changing jobs can have a lasting impact on your life. If you feel like you need to make a decision right away, don't do it alone. Talk to someone you trust. But if you can, it's best to wait until you feel more sure and clear-headed before making any big choices.

Pretending everything's fine, bottling up your feelings, and shutting people out won't help when you're grieving. I tried doing that, and let me tell you, it didn't work out well. Sure, I looked fine on the outside, but inside, I was a mess. It made me feel sick and made it tough to make good choices or connect with others. I'm not saying you must share with anyone if you're not ready. But here's the thing: talking about how you feel isn't just okay—it's a big part of feeling better. It can also help you figure out who you are now that grief is a part of your life.

Get creative—it's a mood lifter, even if you don't think of yourself as an artist. Try journaling or get artsy with painting, drawing, or sculpting. Dancing or diving into DIY projects like gardening or redecorating can also boost your spirits.

Honoring your loved one can bring comfort. Frame special photos of them and hang them on the wall. I made a shadow box with pictures and personal items that belonged to my dad. It's hanging in my office alongside one of my favorite pictures of my mom. You could also plant a tree or garden in your loved one's memory as a living tribute.

Grief affects both the heart and the body, so prioritize self-care. Rest well, move your body, and eat right. If you aren't sleeping well at night, take afternoon naps. If your appetite isn't quite there, try eating small, healthy snacks. Even a leisurely walk with the dog can do wonders. And, if you don't have your own dog, do like me, and borrow the neighbor's dog.

Be mindful of how much and how often you're drinking alcohol. A glass now and then might be okay for some people, but overdoing it can cause a host of new problems. Trying to numb your feelings with alcohol, drugs, or prescription pills can intensify the pain and sadness.

Special dates like anniversaries, birthdays, and holidays can bring up a lot of emotions. Use this time to celebrate the person you've lost. For example, I post birthday tributes to my parents on my Facebook account along with pictures of our happy times to celebrate and honor them. If you're struggling with a specific tradition, talk with family and friends. Maybe you can create a new tradition to mark a special occasion.

Grief changes you. It has certainly changed me. The people we were before are not the people we are today. That doesn't mean we have to feel down all the time. Living fully means embracing all our emotions. Integrating the grief into our new selves opens space for joy, laughter, and connection. Healing isn't about forgetting—it's about finding a way to live from the scar and not the wound.

As a certified Master Life Coach, author, and ordained reverend, Laura E Summers commands a space where individuals transcend their limitations and soar to new heights.

Co-creator of the bestseller *Women Who Rise*, and with certifications from the prestigious Ford Institute and Levin Life Coach Academy, she wields a formidable arsenal of coaching modalities.

Laura is on a relentless quest for mastery, currently pursuing certification as an Art Therapy Practitioner. Her journey began at Aims College, where she honed her skills in broadcast communications.

Yet, Laura's true passion lies in guiding others. Specializing in developing personal action plans, dispelling limiting beliefs, and navigating grief, she empowers her clients to craft their destinies with precision and purpose.

When not working, you'll find Laura challenging herself on the golf course, painting, and spending time with Donnie, her husband and best friend of more than thirty years.

For those ready to embark on a journey of self-discovery and empowerment, Laura is a beacon of hope. Visit her website or connect with her on social media to begin your transformational odyssey. Embrace the unfolding and step into your greatness alongside Laura E Summers.

Website: www.LauraESummers.com
Email: Laura@LauraESummers.com
Instagram: rev.laurasummers.lifecoach
Facebook: Laura E Summers

## Dad & Mom

# LOSS AND FOUND: HOW I LOST IT ALL AND FOUND MYSELF

*By Lolita Taylor*

I lost my job in September.

It's crazy that of all the other losses I've experienced in my life, the loss of my job is what inspired me to write about grief. It wasn't the loss of my grandmother, my divorce, or any of the other losses I've experienced. But the loss of my job, my freedom, and my livelihood took me to a dark place.

Facing the loss of my job made me look at my life and all the losses I've had up to this point, and I realized that my whole life has been filled with it. It's hard for me to talk about because I go through life pretending I have it all. I have a decent home, I take pretty good care of myself, I travel at my leisure, attend concerts, and hang out with my friends and family. Many regard me as the life of the party! I'm always looking to entertain, and I love to have a good time.

My great grandmother used to call me Smiley. She would call me and say, "Hey Smiley," and of course I would just smile. I miss those phone calls. I miss hearing her voice.

This brings me to the easy part of my experience with loss. Losing people is hard, but it's been my experience that it's easier for me to process those than most of the other losses I've experienced. You see, when someone dies, you don't take it as a personal failure. Put another way: it's not anything I can control. So when I lost my great grandmother, my grandmother, my grandfather, numerous aunts and uncles, and two very good childhood friends, it hurt but I was able to process it as the circle of life and do what I needed to do to push through and move on.

I could only imagine what would have happened had I experienced a bigger loss like that of a parent or a child. Honestly, the most palpable loss I experienced was with losing my grandmother because she was my person, and even that I was able to process because she was sick and she was sixty-nine and not happy anymore. Even though sixty-nine isn't old, her quality of life had diminished and quite honestly she didn't want to be here anymore like she was. So although I miss her terribly and I talked to her often and I often ask myself how different my life would be if my grandmother was here, I'm able to push through, and I don't carry guilt. I don't feel like I'm the cause of her not being here.

My biological father's death was a different type of loss. I think I only saw him three or four times in my life. My most vivid memory is of him taking me to what used to be one of the best pizza places in the city and getting me lasagna. I think I was around eight years old in the third grade. I didn't see him again until over thirty years later at his mother's funeral.

He tried reaching out and getting people to contact me because he wanted to try to form a relationship with his one and only daughter, but at the time I was fresh through my divorce. I was still so raw from the pain and disappointment of a failed marriage that I did not have it in me to explore a relationship with a man I'd never known. I didn't trust him. So I told everyone, "You know, thank you, but no thank you. I'm not ready right now."

So two years later, when I got the news that he had passed away, I wasn't sure how to feel. I wasn't grieving because I guess you can't grieve what you never had, but I did feel lost because it was the loss of an opportunity. It was the loss of time, and the loss of becoming Daddy's little girl—something I've never been and always wanted to be. So in this case, instead of grief, I felt guilt. I often think about how things might have been different had I opened up to him. Maybe he would have been here visiting me and not have ended up dead in his apartment.

But the loss that really affects me is the loss no one else sees. Some refer to it as ambiguous loss—the loss of a thing. It is not the mind-blowing heart-wrenching loss of a person that you know you'll never see again. But for me, the loss of my marriage, the loss of my job, the loss of my ability to interact with my mother, and the loss of control over my children are things that I grieve more than any one person.

I know. That's crazy, right? I keep everything. I have outfits probably thirty-plus years old. I have knickknacks from my grandmother and great grandmother and mother that are probably fifty-plus years old. My son says I'm a hoarder, but I think I just take care of things. I don't pile these things up. They're displayed for everyone to see, and I love having things around me that remind me of people I have lost.

The downside to keeping things that I am emotionally attached to is the pain and loss that I experience when they break. Crazy glue has become a great asset! However, there are times when glue doesn't work, and I am forced to put it in the trash.

I've experienced a sense of loss over things that I've never experienced when losing people. Things belong to us. We control things. It's up to us to take care of our things and keep them safe. So when my things become lost or damaged or broken, it hurts. It hurts because it is evidence that I don't have any control over anything. Some people would say that losing a person should prove this for me. But I know you can't depend on people. I should be able to depend on myself. I am responsible for keeping my things safe and I pride myself on that. I know my kids are not my things, but I feel like my loss of control over how they move in this world is related to my loss of control when my things are lost or damaged or broken.

Much like my things, my children are my responsibility. My job is to keep them from harm. Losing the ability to affect their well-being creates a loss of control that I didn't realize I was not ready for. So, really, the thing I don't like to lose the most is control.

The funny thing is how do you miss what you never really had in the first place. What do I really control?

The loss of position—or as I see it, my station in life—has been extremely difficult for me to process. For many years, I was a single mom working two to three jobs to take care of my son. Then I transitioned to being a wife and also having a daughter. I went back to school and got my undergraduate degrees and then my master's degree and finally landed what I thought was my dream job.

So fast forward to today, I am again a single mother, divorced and unemployed. I went from making nearly six figures to food stamps and Medicaid in the span of six months. Everyone tells me it's going to be OK, and deep down inside I know it will be. I know that I'll find a new job and everything will work itself out eventually.

However, that does not mitigate the experience of losing control of my destiny. I took for granted that I would always be OK. I would always have my mobility, so I would always be able to work, and as long as I could work, I'd be able to pay my bills and take care of myself.

But these last six months have scared the hell out of me. My tennis elbow is flaring up, causing me to nearly become disabled. I haven't had any luck finding a job although I've been looking now for almost six months. I've had to borrow money to pay my bills and all of my credit cards are maxed out. I'm terrified. I'm out of control. And no one knows it. I still keep my house clean. I still take care of myself physically. I still get out when I can. I've even taken two cruises since being off work. What they don't see is this black hole inside of me that's filled with doubt, dread, disappointment, and desperation.

I realize that the way my experience with loss has affected me the most is my desire to control everything. Ultimately, my biggest loss is the control that I never had. Realizing that I don't control anything and that I just have to go with the flow of the universe is a paradigm shift in the way I live my life. My new life hack is choosing to accept loss in whatever form it shows itself. I did not realize that giving up my desire to control everything would allow me to find myself. I still fight the urge to run the world. But waking up every day with nowhere to go and no one to talk to is a stark, daily reminder that I have no control. I am lost, and I've been forced to accept my world and my life as it is today.

That acceptance requires me to get to know this person that I have become. Who am I? What am I without all the things I thought I needed to survive?

I am the best kind of lost because I am blessed with the ability to stop and look at where I am and what got me here, as well as decide where I want to go and how to get there. I do that realizing that the route that I take isn't up to me. I can choose a destination, but not the path to getting there. The universe will choose what I have to lose and what I have to learn to get there.

I'm still on my healing journey, but I can say that giving up the control I thought I had has allowed me to gain control over myself that I never had before. I will never be a Daddy's girl. But my daughter is. I miss my grandmother so much, but I can talk to her, and I still have clothes and jewelry and knickknacks that belong to her that I can cherish and pass on to my daughter one day. I'm not able to have the relationship with my mother that my girlfriends have with their mothers due to her issues with bipolar disorder and dementia, but she is still here. I do have a mother, so I just celebrate the time that I do get to spend with her and try to make sure I leave her knowing that she's loved and she's cherished by me at all times.

I'm working on me. I'm working on letting go of my desire to control all things and allowing the universe to chart my path. I've lost so much, yet there is so much more to gain. I look forward to seeing what else the universe brings into my life and the lessons it will teach me.

 Lolita Taylor is a middle-aged divorcée with two adult children and a cat, aka a "Cat Lady." She enjoys taking walks, traveling, and reading, and is a proud graduate of Wayne State University with an MBA in marketing and international business. She is honored to be part of this anthology, and hopes to use her writing to impact and inspire others.

# A SIBLING'S JOURNEY

By Jason Wendroff-Rawnicki

In the summer of 1998, my wife and I took a vacation to Cape May, New Jersey. On the second day of our trip, we took a bicycle ride to explore the town. When we returned to our bed and breakfast, the innkeeper was standing on the porch. He handed me a note to call my parents. As I dialed the number, I had the thought that my grandmother must have died. When my dad picked up the phone, I could hear my mom screaming in the background. Feeling confused, I asked, "Did Grandma die?" Numbly, my father answered, "It's Lauren, she was in a car accident, she's dead."

My sister was dead. The color drained from my body and I went numb. Luckily, my wife was there to keep me from falling down.

After the funeral, I spent a week at my parents' house sitting shiva. During these seven days of remembrance, when family and friends stopped by, I kept hearing, "How are your parents doing?" "Be strong for your parents." "Your parents are going to need you now more than ever."

Why did no one ever ask how I was doing? I felt increasingly forgotten. These statements filled my brain to the point that I began to question the validity of my own grief. So, I pushed all the feelings down and avoided my grief altogether.

I've heard it said that "When you lose a parent, you have lost your past; when you lose a spouse, you have lost your present; when you lose a child, you lose your future. When you lose a sibling, you lose all three."

I had always seen myself growing old with my sister in my life, and, in an instant, that vision was gone. Here I was, twenty-six years old, married for two years, and trying to figure out who I was becoming, and *BAM!* In the space of one phone call, my expectations for the future and the person I dreamed of becoming immediately changed forever. Yet, based on what others were saying to me, dealing with my own grief was secondary to being strong for my parents. So where was I supposed to go from here?

I couldn't go to my parents because they were dealing with their own grief. And on top of "me needing to be strong for them," they emotionally disappeared from my life. Within the first year of Lauren's death, they even tried to force me to grieve the same way they were grieving, and dragged me to a peer support meeting. I attended a few meetings and realized that all the siblings in the group had experienced their loss within the last year. No one there had any long-term experience with grief, so it was the blind leading the blind. I quickly realized those meetings were not going to help me. But the more I pushed down or avoided my grief, the more I struggled. So, I started to look for outside support.

The first thing that I thought of trying was therapy. But, back in 1998, there were really only two options—psychoanalysis and Cognitive Behavioral Therapy. How were either of those going to help me? I already knew *why* I was feeling the way I was feeling. And I also knew my behaviors had shifted because Lauren died. I didn't need more theory; I needed tools. So I decided to take my mental, emotional, and physical health into my own hands.

I started by looking at some of the things that I was already doing, like yoga. The physical practice of yoga helped me understand where the grief lived in my body and how to ease the tension in my muscles and joints. Once I was feeling better *in* my body, it occurred to me that I needed to consider what I was putting *into* my body. This led me to making lifestyle changes around my food choices and proper supplementation. To my surprise and relief, I found that with better nutrition, my mental and emotional health improved. It became clear to me that lifestyle choices affect the entire body. I began to realize if I improved the health of my body, it also improved the health of my brain. This is where my body-centered approach to grief started.

Next, I incorporated meditation. I sat quietly and focused on my breath. I gave my mind permission to do what it was going to do. I learned there is no good or bad meditation. If I sank into the darkness, I knew it would be okay. If I focused on the light, that would also be okay. I accepted that whatever came up, came up. Even now, I often struggle with my own thoughts, but with meditation, I can watch my thoughts without attachment.

As my meditation practice evolved, I realized that while I was able to accept my thoughts as they were, my mind was still all over the place. I needed to learn how to focus. *Visualization* helped me to direct my mind and focus my thoughts. I also used it as a way of managing my emotions.

Through the practice of visualization, I began to realize that my brain does not know the difference between when something is imagined or real. In the early stages of my grief journey, I missed Lauren deeply. So I used visualization to connect with her. I would sit on my cushion, close my eyes, focus on my breath, and imagine her sitting next to me. Then we would have a conversation. Often, I would end up crying during the entire interaction. Once I felt complete, I would say goodbye and schedule another time to speak with her. Even though I only saw this in my mind, it felt real. And that was good enough for me.

After I lost my sister, my identity changed. I was not the same person I was before. The more I longed for the past and pushed away reality, the more pain I experienced. I had to accept who I had become and honor my truth moving forward.

But what was my truth? I did not want to be known as the "guy who lost his sister" or a "grief yoga teacher." What I wanted was to explore new strategies to find happiness and joy again, while at the same time, dealing with my grief.

Over the next two decades, I dug deep into personal development and studied different tools to refocus my mind on what I *did* want from life. Early on, I kept this exploration to myself and did not share it with anyone else. I felt alone and isolated.

Then, in 2019, I was teaching yoga at a grief conference when I realized that there was a growing, global community of bereaved siblings that used the conference as a hub to come together to feel less alone. They were laughing, crying, connecting, partying, and having a great time. When I asked a fellow SIB (what we called our fellow bereaved siblings) what the excitement was all about, she told me that there were no resources in her area and it was the only time of the year that she got to talk about her sister with people who understood what she was going through.

I was dumbfounded. I found it ridiculous that bereaved siblings only talked about their grief three days out of the year, especially with all the fantastic technology we had at our fingertips. It was in that moment that I decided to create SIBS Online, a bereaved sibling peer support group. (Go to www.somaticgrieftherapy.com or www.siblingisland.com for more information.)

All of this internal exploration helped me process my grief and accept the new reality I faced after my sister died. Once I accepted that the person I was before Lauren's death was gone, I had to decide what my new future was going to look like. As my weekly SIBS support group started to grow, I was reminded of the gap that exists in the mental health field. So many "talk" therapists do not understand how to deal with grief, never mind a bereaved sibling. Also, working with the SIBS made me realize how few grievers talked about taking care of their bodies through basic things like sleep, diet, and movement. In fact, many bereaved people turn to harmful behaviors to dull their pain. I decided to get off the sidelines and help grieving people find hope and joy again by taking care of their bodies and increasing their vitality.

Now I knew what my future was going to look like, but how was I going to get there? I had a wide range of gifts and talents I needed to tie together: psychology, therapy, yoga, energy healing, essential oils, healthy lifestyle, diet, and personal development. I spent the next six months restructuring my business from being focused on yoga to offering grief support. I knew I had to develop new skills and capabilities to create a greater impact. I also knew that in order to get different results, I needed to do things differently. If people weren't talking about the importance of the body in managing grief, I had to lead that conversation.

That was the origin of Somatic Grief Therapy. Generally, people only talk about their mental OR physical health—but not both. As a Somatic Grief Therapist, I look at the relationship between the body, the heart, and the mind. I look at grief management from the body up and the mind down. We have to take care of the body so the mind can work efficiently (body up). And, we have to be deliberate with our thoughts because thoughts are vibrations and affect every cell in the body (mind down).

Even small shifts can make a big change. What is the smallest, incremental change you can make to take care of your body right now? Maybe you drink one more ounce of water per day, eat an apple instead of a cookie, or sleep an extra hour per night. The key is to make it easier to accomplish the behaviors you *want* to do, and make it harder to engage in the actions you want to eliminate. For example, if you want to eat healthier, put a bowl of apples on the counter and put the cookies in the back of the pantry.

Next, when you feel the waves of emotion rising, accept them as they are instead of pushing them away or letting them swallow you up. Take three deep breaths and try observing them without judgment. Emotions are simply energy *in motion*. They are meant to *move through* you to heal you. When you fight against your feelings, they will keep repeating themselves until you have processed them and released them.

Then, you also need to understand that you cannot go backward. It is likely you are very different than the person you were before your loss. So use your mind to visualize the person you *want* to be and the life you *want* to live *now*. Remember, you are brave. You are strong. You are resilient. And most importantly, you are alive.

As I've embraced the bereaved sibling part of myself, I've begun to realize that many gifts were born out of my grief. Before Lauren's death, I wasted a lot of time on things that did not matter. Afterward, I realized that time is one of our most precious resources, so I need to make it count. I choose to live life twice as much now, because I'm living it for both of us. Before her passing, I never saw myself as doing anything other than working a boring 9-5 job for someone else, staying for the stable income and benefits, and feeling like I was dead inside. Since then, I've had the courage to break out on my own and do something that creates a positive impact.

Before, I was only focused on myself. Now, I use my gifts to help others. I am also committed to telling people how I feel, so I don't miss that opportunity. My capacity for emotion and compassion have been elevated to whole new level.

In short, I decided to be the change I wanted to see in the world. I realized that if I wanted more people to be grief literate, I needed to educate people on how I want to be treated. If I wanted bereaved siblings to be validated, I needed to tell my story. If I wanted people to stop looking at grieving people as fragile, I needed to show how strong and resilient I am. Many people say that they would do anything to have their person back. I would love to have my sister back, but **ONLY** if I was also able to keep all the lessons that I have learned from her death.

Change, whether internal or external, is not going to happen all at once. Be happy with tiny, incremental shifts, no matter how small or insignificant they might seem. If you expect the change to happen immediately, then the gap between where you are and where you want to be is too big to bridge, and causes frustration and overwhelm. Remember, even a one-percent improvement, every single day, compounds over time.

I could have continued feeling sad, alone, and as though Lauren's car accident had killed us both, but it wouldn't bring her back. I can't change that fact. Instead, I choose to focus on expanding my happiness and joy every day. It is how I celebrate her memory and honor the gift of time that I have been given. Remember, time is our most precious resource. Use it wisely.

 Jason Wendroff-Rawnicki is a Somatic Grief Therapist, keynote speaker, author, and certified yoga educator with a master of arts in psychology. He is also a dōTERRA Essential Oil Gold Leader, and is passionate about facilitating transformation and committed to empowering individuals and families with simple and effective tools to naturally manage their mental, emotional and physical health.

An entrepreneur and business owner since 2000, and cofounder of Shine Yoga Center in New Jersey, Jason draws on over twenty years of experience living a holistic lifestyle—incorporating yoga, meditation, essential oils, healthy eating, conscious communication and authentic relationships to help guide others to a place of greater joy and self-awareness so they can make healthier and more fulfilling choices in their lives. He travels nationally and internationally, leading classes, workshops, retreats and educating about the way grief is stored in the body and how to release it.

In June of 1998, he lost his sister Lauren in a car accident. Knowing that he needed more than talk therapy to deal with his grief, Jason turned toward a body-centered approach. Yoga, meditation, mindfulness, a healthy lifestyle, and essential oils became his path towards recovery.

In his Somatic Grief Therapy practice, Jason believes in a physiology first approach when dealing with grief because the issues get trapped in the tissues. When we change our physical state, we have the energy to do the mental and emotional work needed to bring back hope into our lives.

To see Jason's current classes and offerings go to www.somaticgrieftherapy.com or email him at jason@shineyogacenter.com.

# LIVING FOR JAHVON: A JOURNEY OF HOPE AND HEALING

By Lisa Wilson

My son, Jahvon, was born on December 30, 1997. He was such a smart and beautiful baby. When he was growing up, he was always smiling and so full of beautiful light. His grandfather even nicknamed him Smiley.

Jahvon loved being the center of attention and in the spotlight. He was an entertainer from the start. He was extremely creative and hilarious, so we always laughed a lot when he was around. He danced, sang, made up skits, and created videos for his YouTube channel, which he started at nine years old. He also loved documenting his life and constantly asked his poor younger brother, Cameron, and everyone else to follow him around with a video camera. One time he convinced all the neighborhood kids to work together and make a zombie movie. It was epic! He had a way of pulling people together. He was also passionate and laser-focused when he wanted something. For the longest time, skateboarding was all he could talk about, think about, write about and... you get the picture. He lived it and loved it.

Then, in 2012, at fourteen, he developed a rare bone tumor in his right tibia. It would be the first of five tumors that were removed from his body in four separate surgeries over the next two years. I saw the light in him dim each time he had to endure another procedure. To add insult to injury, skateboarding wasn't even a possibility. He fell into a depression, and that along with his exposure to opioids during his illness, opened the door to his experimentation with drugs.

Since he couldn't be on his skateboard anymore, he shifted his focus to music and decided to become a rapper. I must admit, I wasn't the least bit excited about his new passion. But he went into it with the same determination as skateboarding, and I had to respect his perseverance. Over the next few years, he built a fan base and gained notable popularity and fame. I was always shocked when people stopped him to take pictures or ask for his autograph. Several times, his brother and I were stopped by his fans because they thought Cameron was Jahvon. The two of them looked so much alike that they referred to each other as "twin."

I was proud that Jahvon was doing what he set out to do, even if I wasn't always proud of the content and I was concerned about his increasing drug use. It's not always easy to support our kids' dreams, and I had to constantly remind myself that it was his life and I had to let him figure it out. As he got deeper into drugs, he got into a lot of trouble and the darkness within him grew. He was arrested several times and seemed to be spiraling out of control. His addiction often got in the way of his musical progress and caused him to miss many opportunities. Eventually, he decided to try to escape the problems he faced in Florida and moved to California.

There, his popularity as an artist grew, but he couldn't seem to leave the drugs alone. He developed mental illness as a result of his drug use. Occasionally he would suffer from bouts of psychosis, paranoia, and hallucinations that were triggered by certain drugs and when he tried to detox. It was really scary because he would call me in hysterics and tell me outrageous stories about the situations he was in. Sometimes he would be lost or not know where he was. I was so far away. What was I supposed to do? How was I supposed to help him? Most of the time he wouldn't even remember that he had called, but I struggled to forget.

At the same time, I was trying to live my own life and not self-destruct. Being the parent of an addict comes with constant worry. The only way I could experience peace was to practice detachment. That meant allowing the consequences of his actions to belong to him and loving him without feeling like I needed to own or change his behavior. It was so difficult to do and it was exhausting. My son was robbed, beaten up, and even stabbed during the time he lived in California. In the weeks leading up to his death, we spoke at length about his addiction. For the first time, he was open about it and acknowledged how much it tormented him. He told me it was a daily fight that sometimes he would win and sometimes he wouldn't. He told me about how ashamed it made him feel and how much he wanted to be better.

On Wednesday, August 11 at 6:13 p.m., I got a phone call from Jahvon while I was making dinner. He sounded confused and disoriented, and I proceeded to do what I always do when he called in that state—I fussed at him. He stopped me to say, "You know you are the most beautiful person to me, right Mom?"

*What a strange thing to say*, I thought. I put down the knife that was in my hand. "Is everything okay?" I asked.

"I love you, Mom. I just needed you to know that." He repeated it two more times before hanging up the phone.

That was the last phone call my son made before taking his own life. His body was found five days later. He was labeled a John Doe until he could be identified with bone records. It was such a sad ending to my beautiful son's life—a life that was full of potential but also full of pain.

The moment I received the phone call about his death was like a bomb blast. I was vaporized! It took months for me to start to want to live again. I needed to be okay for my son, Cameron, who had just lost his brother and was also devastated. And I still had a life full of responsibilities that didn't stop just because my heart was shattered.

I realized that no amount of time, tears, screams, or prayers would change reality. My son was gone. By accepting that fact, I was able to start to navigate through the many emotions associated with my grief. You see, I had already shed so many tears, for such a long time, for my precious child. So even though the reality of the situation was crushing, a part of me was at peace for the first time in a long time. I was not worried about Jahvon and whether he was struggling or not. I wasn't thinking about the turmoil he experienced as he rode the roller coaster of addiction and mental illness. We weren't fighting or arguing. He wasn't confused or tormented. My son was finally at peace. There was another part of me that was very angry and hurt by his poor choices and how they had affected all of us. How could he leave us like this? I had thought there would be time for him to turn it around and get better. But it was his life and it wasn't up to me.

Being a survivor of suicide loss comes with many mixed emotions and unanswered questions. It is similar to how I felt as the parent of an addict. My son was always killing himself—he was just doing it slowly. I felt the pain of losing him over and over, each time he succumbed to the drugs. Dealing with this kind of trauma can be a lonely and difficult road for parents. There's so much judgment and misunderstanding associated with addiction, mental illness, and suicide.

Judgment aside, I want others to understand that my son was a beautiful person even though he struggled. He was so much more than his addiction. His life mattered and he was loved even though he was flawed. He was talented, funny, creative, and so full of life. He had dreams and goals and worked hard to accomplish them. He wanted to be sober and a role model for his brother. He wanted to be famous and make sure his family was taken care of. He hated himself for everything he was that hurt his family and that got in the way of his success. Families that are dealing with addiction and or mental illness need support, not judgment!

So now what? I am left with a lot of unanswered questions, my memories, and my grief. I am also left in the land of the living. Left picking up the pieces. Left with the responsibility to heal and learn how to live again. I am also left with choices about what that will look like. How I proceed is my choice. Grief is a journey that is not linear. There isn't a roadmap to follow and every day will look different.

At first, I felt scattered and had a difficult time concentrating. Sometimes, I would find myself gasping for air all of a sudden, not realizing I had been holding my breath. I cried more than I had ever cried in my life. I couldn't be alone for more than ten minutes without the tears starting to flow. After the first year, I got frustrated because I still felt like a stranger to myself and craved returning to "normal." I have come to understand that I am a new person and returning to "normal" is not an option. I get to define what that will be like. From the start, I made sure to give myself grace and permission to allow my grief to not have parameters. My goal, as it has always been, is to be well and to live an abundant and joyful life. Some days I get close and other days are far from it. I just have to keep moving forward.

Nothing has changed in terms of him being gone, but I have learned so much since the day that bomb went off in my life. I learned that grief cannot be ignored and it doesn't go away. It is something you learn to live with. What helped me the most is making space for my grief. This is intentional time I set aside to grieve. Making space doesn't always look the same. Sometimes I go to the beach and sit alone by the ocean. Other times, I go for a long drive or walk. Some days I look at pictures or videos of Jahvon and get lost in my memories for a while. I allow the tears to flow or feel whatever comes up in that moment, but I intentionally sit in it. I don't run from it. I also make space by meeting with my therapist and learning strategies to help my healing. I also like to listen to his music and write in my journal. Space can be having lunch with friends who can relate. It can even be a vigorous workout with my headphones on. I do whatever I want or need to do at that time.

In the beginning, my grief occupied a lot of space. Now, it takes up less as I learn to navigate life without my son. I have accepted his absence and I have shifted my energy to deciding how I can live in his honor. I use the proceeds from his music to support organizations that support at-risk youth programs and suicide prevention. I talk about him and to him often because he lives in me and through me.

My life will always be separated into before and after, and every holiday and milestone will be bittersweet, but I know my son is watching and I know he would want me to LIVE. For that reason, I will seek joy in every day and I will LIVE because I can. As difficult as that is at times, I will live for my son, Jahvon!

 Lisa is a wife and mother of two boys with seventeen years of experience in education. She has dedicated her life to fostering growth and resilience in others. Her journey as a survivor of suicide loss has profoundly influenced her mission to advocate for families facing barriers and trauma, offering them the support and empathy they need to heal.

As part of her grief journey, she became a certified personal trainer and nutrition coach, initially to help herself and then to help others. She is passionate about inspiring others to embrace positivity and self-care, believing that wellness and nutrition are foundational to a fulfilling life. Her goal is to educate, encourage, and empower individuals to lead healthier, happier lives through holistic wellness practices.

When she isn't exercising or enjoying the outdoors with her husband, Shawn, and dog, Marlo, she's reading a new book or listening to music while writing in her journal. Finding balance in life and making space for the important work of healing is a huge part of who she is.

# THE PHONE RANG

*By Camille Woods*

$\mathcal{S}$ometimes I think back and my fantasy is that the phone never rang, that we got up that morning and headed out to see a childhood friend at a local museum as planned. I dream that my son, Marcus, had in fact taken the late bus at the end of the following week and had driven home with us, just like we had discussed the night before.

When I woke up on July 6, 2014, all was right with the world. We were far from our Belleville, Michigan home, having traveled to Tuscaloosa, Alabama, for my daughter Mayceeclair's summer dance camp with the American Ballet Theater. She had just finished the first week of a three-week session at the prestigious school. While she slept soundly in the next room, I relaxed as the sun blazed through the window.

The phone rang.

I remember answering and hearing my bonus son, my fiancé's child David, say, "The police came here and I was too scared to answer the door."

I don't know if I asked him any other questions; I just remember thinking I should call Belleville's finest and find out what they wanted. When the woman on the other end of the line told me that an officer would call me back momentarily, I don't recall having any worrisome feelings. I just waited for the return call.

The phone rang.

"Good morning, are you Camille Woods?" a male voice asked. I assured him I was. "My name is Officer Buxton. Are you the parent of Marcus McIntosh?"

"Yes, what did he do?" I asked. He'd never been in trouble before, but why else would an officer be seeking me out?

"Ma'am, do I understand that you are currently in Alabama?"

"Yes, I am—"

"Is there anyone with you?" he asked.

"My thirteen-year-old daughter and I are here for a ballet camp… what's wrong?" I asked, worry creeping into my voice.

"There was a car accident last night that involved your son Marcus."

I sat up on the edge of the bed and suddenly the sun did not seem as bright. I felt as if my stomach was on the floor. "Is he ok?!" I hollered into the phone.

"Ma'am, I regret to inform you that your son is deceased."

*I regret to inform you that your son is deceased. I REGRET to inform you that your son is deceased. I regret to inform YOU that your son is deceased. I regret to inform you that your son is DECEASED.*

I have heard those words in my head a million times since that morning, and there has never been any difference in how they sound. No matter where the emphasis lies—it is horror. It is unimaginable. It is the nightmare every parent pretends will never happen to them.

I began screaming. "Are you sure?! No! No! I just spoke to him at midnight! Are you sure?!"

My daughter came running into the room. "What's wrong?" she asked, grabbing my arm, a look of terror on her face. She asked me over and over again as I continued to scream. Finally, with no reservation or compassion or kindness or sense of control, I screamed at the top of my lungs, "YOUR BROTHER IS DEAD!"

I find myself reliving that moment.

*The phone rang.*

Eight hours later, after calling everyone I knew to tell them my son was gone, I still sat in the same spot on the floor.

My beautiful, amazing Marcus. My firstborn. My entire soul. My best friend. My protector. My hero. My everything. Was gone.

As I made the calls and heard everyone's screams on the other end of the line, I found myself sinking deeper and deeper—into a space where everything was unknown to me. By the time my older brother, Jeff, arrived from Michigan to drive us home, I had cried so that my eyes were nearly swollen shut. Still, the tears poured down.

My daughter held my hand as we walked out of the apartment and attempted to sooth me by saying, "Marcus would have held you like this."

The interminable twelve-hour drive home was mostly silent. Jeff drove through the night, nonstop, listening to me sob and beg the universe to return Marcus to me.

The process of laying a child to rest is unthinkable. First, there was the identification of his body, where I sat in a small room and his face suddenly appeared on a television screen. When a nameless woman handed me my son's "belongings," it was just a small envelope with his earrings inside. I asked, "Where are his phone? His shoes?" The woman said she didn't know.

The next stop was the funeral home, where I asked a lovely woman named Judy to bring my son to me immediately. I needed to see him before they did anything to him. "No embalming, no fake makeup," I begged, "Just my Marcus." She promised to have him with me the next day.

When Maycee and I returned home, there was a crowd of neighbors and friends standing in my yard, all of them crying. As I made my way into our small home, Marcus's closest and dearest friend, Ethan, fell into my arms and simply said, "He was my brother." I had no words for him.

Everyone wanted to help. Everyone wanted to fix it, but my grief was beyond fixing. The next six days were a blur of phone calls, family reaching out, and well-meaning people bringing food. I called it the grief buffet. My fiancé helped me out of bed each morning. In the midst of all of this was my daughter, who I could not attend to. I think back on that and wish I could have done more to soothe her. But I have to admit, I was lost.

There are many things I have no memory of. Even today, my brain still protects me and keeps those memories at bay. I am told that when we walked into the funeral home to see him, I fell to my knees… twice. I don't recall that. I don't recall the service, or the fact that I spoke at the event. I don't remember what I did when they closed his casket that last day, on July 12. I don't remember the one thousand people who came to see him through the visitation and service. One thousand.

I do recall Judy, the lovely funeral director, keeping her promise to let me see him the day after we had arrived home. She called me and said simply, "He is here."

I raced to the funeral home and was taken downstairs to a large room. Across the room, a huge white bag rested on a long metal table. My 6'4, 380 lb. son was in that bag. As I walked over, I asked Judy to unzip it so I could see my baby. Judy looked down and said, "I can't do that." She had removed my son's left arm from the bag prior to my arrival and that was all I could see.

"Why? I need to see all of him!" I said harshly.

Judy explained that my beautiful Marcus had been given an autopsy and shouldn't be seen as he was not "prepared." My mind still couldn't comprehend this idea, but I understood she would not unzip that bag.

I took that hand and kissed it and held it for what seemed like hours. I poured tears onto it and smelled him and studied the way his fingers were slightly curved like mine. I squeezed the chubby part of his arm and recalled what it had been like to kiss those arms when he was a chubby toddler. I loved that arm and hand with every part of me. I will always be grateful to Judy for creating that space for me to be with him, in the only way I had left.

Time moves on, they say. Loved ones are buried or cremated, and time moves on. But the time for me was endless.

For five years, I fought the court system to place the driver of the car that stole my son in prison. I drove to the intersection where it happened almost weekly, and waited for the garbage trucks to drive by, hoping I'd have the strength to pull out in front of one. But I was never able to do it. I felt weak because I wanted to die too. I wanted to be with him. Why couldn't I just do it? There was nothing this Earth could offer me to replace the soul that had been taken. The hopelessness in the dark abyss that was me was palpable. I drank every night.

One evening after downing my second bottle of wine, I fell asleep, or more likely, I passed out. I woke up, unable to breathe, choking on my own vomit. I fell out of my bed onto the floor and fought to take in air. I coughed and hacked and fought for my life. In that moment, I realized I didn't want to die. It was the wakeup call I needed to bring some light into the darkness.

Over the next few years, I took that light and my son's legacy and created a program that allowed me to share him with the students I worked with and the rest of the community. Project "I Got You. –Big Mack" was born in April 2016. Each October, which is nationally known as National Bullying Awareness Month, we celebrate being pro-kindness instead. Project "I Got You" asks students to perform acts of kindness. Each act is an "I Got You," and they know that these are the words my son, Marcus (also known as Big Mack), often said while taking care of others. The children earn a push pin with each act, which is then placed in a wreath. To date, it has been seven years since my son's passing, and over 10,000 acts of kindness have been performed.

I've begun a food pantry and a holiday family adoption program as well. I sold T-shirts with *I Got You* −*Big Mack* printed on them to fund it all. My son's simple message has traveled to eight countries via the ambassadors who wore those shirts. My son's legacy of love and kindness lives on in people that never met him. It brought me back to life and gave me a reason to live. Because he couldn't. It also showed me the way back to a place where I could care for Mayceeclair. I wasn't lost. I was finding my way.

As I move into the tenth year since my son left (I loathe the word "died"), I find myself searching for new ways to honor him and live my life as full as possible. This summer, I will swim a one mile race on July 12, to honor him on the day I laid him to rest.

I will find a new memory for that day. I will breathe in and out for him, because he can't. Don't get me wrong, I still wish I'd never heard the phone ring.

There are still days when the pain is so harsh that I feel like I can't make it, but I know that I have to. I get up. I dress. I breathe. I exist. I know it's Marcus who helps me do this. It's on those tough days when I hear his voice in my head, saying, "C'mon, Ma, I got you." In that moment, he gives me strength.

After all, the strength is in the living, not the dying.

Camille is a licensed school social worker, private practice clinical therapist, storyteller, and Moth Story Hour Two-time Grand Slam winner, through which her storytelling has been featured on National Public Radio.

Camille is also the founder of Project "I Got You. –Big Mack," an educational program and winner of Washtenaw County Project of the Year in 2018. She is dedicated to sharing her son's legacy of giving and kindness with today's youth, and helping them understand what it means to say "I Got You" through acts of kindness. Her program has accomplished over 10,000 acts of kindness to date.

Camille is married and the mother to her beautiful daughter, Mayceeclair, bonus son David, and "Grammy Cammy" to David's two daughters, Eva and Naomi. Family means everything to Camille, and losing her son Marcus taught her that every moment must be lived to the fullest. You can find Camille in the pool swimming laps, listening to 70s easy listening, basking in the sun in the summer by Lake Michigan, or at the local public pool she calls the "Rutheford Resort."

# FINDING SMILES

By Sassy Ruth

## Me & Mommy

My mom tells people that I snuggle on my own terms. The truth is — she tosses and wiggles around so much in bed it's impossible to get any rest!

But I humor her and let her believe. She's been through enough. *We've* been through enough.

From the moment we met, I knew it was *my job* to take care of mommy. She rescued me after she lost her first baby, Harlie. I rescued her from the pain of that loss.

My life before mommy was miserable. It made me afraid of practically everyone.

And everything. Noises. Objects. Being alone.

The people at the shelter said I wasn't friendly. They took my fear to mean that I'm angry. "Aggressive," they told mommy. But mommy saw right through that story. She understood... me and the entire situation.

She knew I just needed some comfort. Time to adjust. Time to sniff things. And with all of the patience in the world, mommy taught me how to survive in this big, noisy world.

Just like I knew she would — from that very first moment. We're connected. In ways most of the world doesn't understand.

I can tell before she can when she's not ok. And in all fairness, she knows when I'm not ok too. Even when I try to pretend that everything is fine so mommy won't worry, she knows.

We're connected. We have been since that first moment... when she was sitting on the floor crying — and I crawled in her lap to lick her nose.

## Sassy

I was born in Michigan sometime during the winter of 2012. My fur mommy and all of my siblings and I were together, but no one paid any attention to us.

If we cried, they yelled. If we barked, they threw things. Thankfully, someone reported these mean people, and we were all rescued and taken to the shelter where mommy found me.

We got to stay together at first, but people started coming and taking my brothers and sisters. One by one. No one looked at my fur mommy, who seemed so sad. And the people at the shelter had told visitors that I was aggressive, remember?

I hated it.

Until mommy walked in.

And almost immediately, she burst into tears. But something changed when I crawled in her lap. I made her feel better. I made her smile, even if it was through her tears.

And I knew my job was to always take care of my new mommy. To make her happy. To keep her safe.

## Mommy

We take care of each other. Our entire first week together, mommy held me through the night and let me sleep on her chest.

I'm not even sure if she slept. If I heard a scary sound or had a bad dream, she was comforting me immediately.

And I rescued mommy at her lowest point. She still put everything else aside to take care of me.

Neither one of us knew there would be so many more lows, including the lowest of lowest possible points.

But even without knowing this, I knew mommy was always a little bit sad. She smiled and laughed and other people might not have seen what I knew was always there, just beneath the surface.

## Mommy & Me
She cried to me and let me lick her tears.

We were always together, except when mommy worked. She loves her work. She's so good at it. I got to visit and spend some days with her in her office.

I was so impressed with her dedication to her clients. With her dedication to making a difference.

We spent lots of time on walks and adventures. I was scared at first, but I had mommy to protect me.

I learned to play fetch. Sometimes I wouldn't fetch just to see how funny mommy thought it was that she was doing all the running.

My favorite thing to do is make mommy smile. I also love swimming. Mommy had a little pool in our yard for me, but she also took me to really big pools. I found out later that they're lakes.

It really didn't (and doesn't) matter where mommy takes me. As long as we're together, we're both happy. We're both ok.

Usually, the places mommy takes me are for me. And she's so happy to make me happy.

The day I met daddy for the first time, mommy was excited. She had a different kind of smile. It was an entirely different kind of happy.

We went to this place with loud planes and tons of traffic. Mommy usually hates traffic. She avoids traffic. And I hated all of it.

Except mommy was so happy…
Daddy

He walked towards the car with the biggest grin. All I was thinking was, "Who the hell is this guy?"

Mommy let me sit on her lap up front, and she let this guy drive us home.

It's *our* Car. Why was HE driving?

Then he walked in my house, acting like he owned the place. He was visiting MY house. MY mommy.

But mommy sure was happy around him. I'd never seen her like this before.

So who the hell did this guy think he was — waltzing in here and doing *my* job? I make mommy happy. I decided I'd show him.

Grrrrr — I grabbed his sleeve. He grabbed it back and played tug with me. Huh? Mommy didn't play with me that way. She actually got kind of upset if I tried to play tug with her clothes. She would make me grab a toy.

This guy wasn't doing that.... and I couldn't tell if mommy liked it or not. But I loved it.

Wait. Who the hell *was* this guy? *MY mommy.*

I was so confused.

Daddy came out of nowhere, but then it was like he'd been here all along. The three of us.

I tried to be mad. On his first night visiting, I jumped up on the bed so he couldn't lay next to mommy. He didn't care.

He jumped in next to me and rubbed my belly.

That made mommy even happier. It made it easy to give in.

At first daddy would come and then go. Mommy was sad when he left... but not sad like before.

Then mommy started leaving and I had to go to camp. My friends were fun, but staying there reminded me of the shelter.

I missed mommy.

But she always came to get me, and then daddy would visit again.

He came for a longer visit and something big happened. Mommy was really happy. Everyone was calling and coming over to celebrate.

And this time when daddy left, mommy wasn't really sad. She started getting big boxes that I climbed inside. I even ate one of the boxes, but playing in them was more fun.

Mommy let me. But she started filling them with stuff and the house looked funny. Daddy came and helped put everything in boxes. And people came to take the boxes and some furniture.

Where could I go to get comfy?

I didn't need to think about this very long, because we got in the car (with some boxes, too). Mommy waved bye to our house and before I knew it — we were moving into daddy's house.

Me, Mommy & Daddy

I hated it.

It was loud.

And when mommy took me on walks, there was no grass. Where could I go potty? But we were all together. And mommy was with me wayyyy more.

We went camping and hiking. And swimming. My most favorite activity, and mommy took me lots. Daddy sometimes came with us, but sometimes we went while he was at work.

We moved again. More boxes. But this time it was to a house with a really big yard. And life was so great. We were all so happy. I still took care of mommy, but daddy was there to take care of us both too.

And he did.

Mommy and I were in the scariest car accident. Instinct kicked in and I was ready to take care of mommy. But daddy was on top of it.

So I could relax.

I didn't have to be on guard all of the time, because we had daddy.

I learned to love our Colorado life.

I wasn't alone very much at all. I got to go to all these places. Places where mommy used to leave me in the car when she visited. There were lots of people. Food.

All kinds of dog parks. Even other people's houses. My favorites were the adventures we all went on together.

I settled in. I relaxed. I learned that I didn't have to be on guard all of the time, protecting mommy.

Everything was perfect.

But then, another big day happened — and this time, not the good kind of big day. The worst possible day.

Mommy wasn't ok. I was already helping her recover from back surgery, but something else happened. Mommy was picked up and left in a panic. I paced. She came back with people and everyone was sad. And more people kept coming over.

But not daddy.

No matter how many times I looked...

I heard cars and got excited only to realize they weren't his car coming home.

Daddy never came back home. Mommy was a mess. I didn't leave her side. I was a mess too... but I kicked it into gear to take care of mommy. That's my job.

Again.

Because daddy isn't here.

Me & Mommy

Life got weird. Mommy stayed up at night. She tried to sleep sometimes, but couldn't. So I stayed up with her.

Mommy gave me all of her attention. We spent our days going all over Colorado. I got to swim in so many fun places.

I'd race in the door when we got home hoping daddy was there waiting, but he never was. This seemed to make mommy even more sad.

Lost. We were both completely lost.

We still talked to daddy. We snuggled at night and wrote him letters. It became our special time. But it's not the same.

We talked to daddy in the car.

I'd get excited... expecting to see him. It took me awhile to figure out that we were talking to daddy in a different place.

Mommy says he's always with us and can always hear us, but we don't hear him.

We don't see him. It's not fair and I don't like it. Mommy has been through enough. We've been through enough.

It was the saddest I'd ever seen mommy. I did everything I could think of to make her smile, just like she did everything she could think of to make me smile.

But smiling wasn't happening without daddy. Lots of things weren't happening without daddy. Mommy kept telling me we'd be ok….. but I sure didn't see how.

Grand Lake

Mommy started asking me if I wanted to go to the mountains. We loooove the mountains. Daddy loves the mountains. For some reason, no one else wanted us to go.

Thank goodness mommy took us anyway. It was sad without daddy, but so was everything.

We both made a friend. Mommy hadn't been very interested in anything. Or anyone. Seeing her let someone in made it easier for me to relax. And I played with her new friend's puppy.

But I enjoyed it.

Mommy had been taking me all over to play with friends — but this was the first time I was really enjoying it. And I could see mommy smile a tiny bit. I could tell me being happy is as important to her as her being happy is important to me.

It was a vacation I'll never forget.

We both came home still sad, but a little bit less heavy.

**Dallas**

I was sad leaving my new friend. Mommy promised me that we'd stay in touch and have visits.

I worried that that wouldn't be enough… for either of us! But then mommy told me she was thinking about getting us a puppy. She worried that I'd feel less loved.

I ran in circles trying to tell her that I also wanted a sister. It wouldn't be the same as daddy. Nothing and no one ever can be.

But it was a start. It was something to look forward to instead of thinking about all we'd lost.

After so many months of being so sad, we both enjoyed looking for my perfect sister.

Mommy even asked me to help pick out names. I let her know (with barks) the really bad ones.

And before I knew it, Dallas was here. She was a fuzzy little ball of energy. She made me and mommy laugh, a sound I had forgotten how much I love and need.

I got to teach her how to use the doggy door and how to swim. She was so nervous at first, but now she loves swimming as much as I do.

She follows me everywhere.

I take care of her... But she takes care of us, too. We have our own, new family.

I still wish daddy was here, too, though.

## Me, Mommy & Dallas

We keep daddy with us, always. In conversations. In decisions.

Mommy started doing more. Most things we do all together as our new family, but mommy also started doing things without us.

Before, I hated it when mommy didn't take me. Anywhere.

But now, it just made me happy to see her do anything. She still was so lost without daddy. But at least she was trying to find her way.

She makes me part of every decision. I could hear mommy on the phone talking about wanting to move. She worried that I would be upset.

I found a way to let her know that it was ok. Dallas is happy to do anything. Anywhere. With anyone. So it was up to me. And I gave the ok.

And I could see how hard it was for mommy packing those boxes. She really cried. We talked to daddy in every room. We took pictures.

And as soon as we got to our next home, mommy seemed a little bit lighter.

She decorated differently. She started cooking, which I love. Something usually falls on the ground while she's cooking, and I always get to it before mommy can pick it up. So yummy.

And our move helped mommy come up with her absolute best ideas. Ever.

## Griefhab

I watched mommy go from going through the motions to getting that glimmer back in her eyes. She had a fire inside of her again. One that grows with every day.

Mommy said she needed rehab for grief, and thank goodness a friend told her that was genius. Mommy tells everyone that our weaknesses are actually our superpowers.

She was able to turn this perceived weakness into the biggest gift for so many.

Mommy gets it in ways other people don't. Just like when she ignored the people at the shelter who told her I'm aggressive.

Mommy knew better. She cares about doing what's right. Mommy cares about making a difference. Leaving things better than how we found them.

We've been working on Griefhab together for over four years. Yes — WE. I'm obviously a huge part of Griefhab. We have BIG things to do in this world!

We're working on getting important invisible awareness days legally added to calendars. So the world can provide more support and resources to those in need. We're working on changing bereavement laws. Because only getting 1–3 days is a joke!

I get to go to mommy's retreats and help other people who feel sad smile. Dallas helps, too, but it's just a game to her. It's work to me. Important work.

Sometimes we get to go with mommy when she speaks. We're there to help others, but secretly I'm just so proud of mommy. Of both of us.

We got through the darkest times. Together. And we still miss daddy. We still write to him every night and tell him all about our days. We tell Dallas funny stories and show her our favorite pictures.

But we're not stuck anymore. When we cry, it's usually happy tears. Mommy still lets me lick her tears.

It's my job to take care of her!

## Planting Our Roots

We live in a new area now. Mommy still takes us to our favorite lakes and parks, but we go back home to our quiet place. It's not busy. Or loud. I love it.

We haven't heard those loud sirens in forever. There's not as much for me to worry about here. I still take care of mommy, but I'm not always on guard. I don't have to be.

Mommy is stronger now.

It feels safe. Mommy feels safe.

Who knows what adventures are next. We're always up to something new and fun. Mommy says it's in honor of daddy. We want to make him proud.

Mommy doesn't know that I can talk to daddy sometimes. Every now and then, I even see him watching us. I know he's always here. And he's already so proud of us.

He was worried about mommy for so long, just like I was. And guess what? Now I know that daddy is still here — in a different way. And he still takes care of mommy. He takes care of both of us. And Dallas, too.

Not the way I do. I'm still here to make mommy smile and to take care of her every day. Daddy's always here watching. Guiding us.

I'd rather have him here, playing tug and being silly. But we're going to be ok, the three of us Ruth girls. We have each other. And guess what else? Mommy says we're badasses.

So if you're going through something tough…

If you've lost your favorite person…

If you've moved and have to find places to go potty without grass — I get it. My best advice is not to go through it alone.

That week in the mountains changed everything for us. We let people in. And now we have so many more people. We have Dallas. And we learned that other people mean well, but they don't know what's best!

We do!

We all have to find our own way. And our people. I couldn't get through this without mommy. And she can't get through it without me!

Together, we're better. And we've got BIG things to do! Just you watch.

---

**About Sassy Ruth**

 Sassy is an almost thirteen year old pitbull mix. She's the extremely proud President of Griefhab. Often called Roo or Sassaroo by loved ones because of the way she hops like a kangaroo when excited, Sassy absolutely loves doing anything outdoors, especially swimming.

After unexpectedly losing her daddy, Sassy has been on a mission to not only take care of her mommy, but also anyone else who is struggling through snuggling, kisses, and endless entertainment.

Sassy understands pain. She uses a unique combination of love and humor to help people find their smiles. She guides people to enjoy the simple things, live life to the fullest, and to always remember the importance of playing, resting, and celebrating.

Sassy encourages everyone to be their true selves, to wag their tails and express themselves, to roll in the grass when you're feeling frisky, and to love unconditionally.

In her free time, you can find Sassy with her mom and little sister on one of their outdoor adventures. They love living in Colorado and never miss an opportunity to explore their beautiful surroundings.

You can follow Sassy on social media here:

https://www.facebook.com/sassy.ruth.2024?mibextid =LQQJ4d

And...follow Sassy's paw prints to the next Faces of Grief book — for pet loss!

# ACKNOWLEDGMENTS

This book is made possible by the financial contributions from Griefhab, Samantha Ruth, and all of the authors.

We all care deeply about not only providing support and resources, but also about changing the overall grief culture. We're committed to sharing our stories to break stigmas, raise awareness, and inspire hope.

Thank you for supporting our movement!

A special thank you to Alexa Bigwarfe of writepublishsell.com for embracing and being a part of Faces of Grief.

And a special thank you to Jack Canfield for writing an endorsement on our cover. Your mentorship and support mean everything to me. Without you, none of this would be here. You helped me find my path during my darkest times and reminded me of my own light! I am eternally grateful.

*Hello! I'm Samantha.*
*Please call me Sam.*

My mission is to change the way the world views both grief and mental illness, so people can openly speak about whatever issues they have and get the help they not only need but deserve without fear of judgment, labels, and repercussions.

**GRIEF IS A VERY PERSONAL JOURNEY. BUT YOU DON'T HAVE TO GO THROUGH IT ALONE.**

**INTRODUCING**

*grief*hab™

Griefhab is a totally new approach to grief support services. It's 100% tailored to you and your needs. There's no other program like this. In most grief programs, you have to wait until your next appointment to deal with what's on your mind. Not in Griefhab.

Griefhab eliminates the waiting, the waiting rooms, therapist's agenda...

**THIS IS ABOUT GRIEVING** *your way!*

*Looking for more?*

**JOIN TEAM**

*Ruthless*

Team Ruthless is a place to get UNLIMITED access to me, a Licensed Psychologist, Widow, and expert in running groups!

- Unconditional Support
- EIGHT groups EVERY week PLUS EVERY
- HOLIDAY!
- And then there's our daily chats - as
- many times a day as anyone needs
- Plus BONUS groups with special guests

**HEALING TOGETHER EVENTS**

The world doesn't discuss grief. People think they have to deal with it privately. Griefhab has multiple events throughout the year, with the main event - **Healing Together Through the Holidays,** honoring National Grief Awareness Week. Visit **www.samantharuth.com** to learn more.

# OUR SPONSORS

# Ellen Craine

JD, LMSW-Clinical &
Macro, ACSW, INHC

## Loss and Grief Specialist,

Social Work Consultant, and Trainer

Work with Ellen and join the Facebook community: Living Through Loss and Grief

#1 International Best Selling Author

(248) 539-3850
www.crainecounseling.com
ellen@crainecounseling.com

Listen to grief expert
and widow, Kate
Mollison discuss
navigating life after
losing a spouse.

**The**
**Happily**
**Never After**
**Podcast**

***New episodes***
***every Tuesday***!

*And all major platforms*

J. Lewis III., the CEO of J. Lewis III Motivation, is a podcaster, grief empowerment strategist, author, and speaker who specializes in shifting grievers' perspectives on their present challenges by showing

how the negative energy of hardship can become the catalyst to discoveries of hidden talents and unique gifts. Gifts that have been birthed from the pain of one's grief-related experience.

*J. Lewis's motto is: Transforming Grief Into Fuel*

Mr. Lewis, the creator of The Grief Empowerment Theory, is dedicated to helping people realize that

their challenges' are negative energy that can fuel growth and progress. The Grief Empowerment Theory program, a practical approach developed by J. Lewis, is designed to help clients discover the resilience that can be cultivated through their personal grief experiences.

J. Lewis services the Austin, TX region and worldwide online. Schedule a discovery call today to learn how to use your challenges to your advantage. Understand how grief empowerment can transform negative energy so you can repurpose it into fuel.

# HOW TO WORK WITH
# SAMANTHA/GRIEFHAB

# BECOME AN AUTHOR

## Become a Co-Author in one of the next
## FACES OF GRIEF BOOKS...

*Do you have a story to share?*
*Do You Want To Join Our Movement?*

Help us break stigmas, provide education, and offer support by joining us as a co-author in one of our upcoming books:

**Faces of Grief**: For Addiction and Overdose
**Faces of Grief**: Surviving Pet Loss

**You don't have to be a writer, you just have to want to share your story.**

Publishing a book costs time and money, so please note that there is an investment to participate. These funds go directly to the editing, designing, publishing, and marketing of the books.

You'll have an opportunity to have your own pre-sale as well as many opportunities to earn back your investment BEFORE the book even launches!

There are also several different levels of investment (and payment plans) to choose from.

*Join the Movement!*

**REACH OUT TO:** Samantha Ruth      FOUNDER OF GRIEFHAB

# BECOME A SPONSOR

## Become a *Sponsor!*

THERE ARE SO MANY DIFFERENT WAYS THAT YOU CAN BECOME A SPONSOR

## SPONSOR FACES OF GRIEF - FOR ADDICTION AND OVERDOSE or FACES OF GRIEF - FOR PET LOSS

### Sponsor an Author's Chapter

Help someone who couldn't otherwise be a part of this project. With love or anonymously – your sponsorship will allow someone to share their story and help others!

✓ Feature your brand in our Resources Section

✓ Place an ad in the book's advertising section

### Sponsor the Book and / or Audiobook

✓ Get your logo on the book cover

✓ Get your logo on the audiobook cover

✓ Get your logo on both

✓ **Audiobook Option**: Include your custom commercial within the audiobook

### Sponsor 2025 Healing Together Events

✓ Feature your branding at the events and in all promotions

### Silent Sponsor

Prefer to remain anonymous? Support us without public recognition

## *Be Part of the Change!*

📞 +1 (248) 730-5544          ✉ sam@samantharuth.com

# RESOURCE LIST FOR FACES OF GRIEF

- Books
  - Self-Help
    - Bearing the Unbearable by Joanne Cacciatore
    - Death of a Parent: Transition to a New Adult Identity by Debra Umberson
    - I'm Not a Mourning Person: Braving Loss, Grief, and the Big Messy Emotions That Happen When Life Falls by Kris Carr
    - Broken Open: How Difficult Times Can Help Us Grow by Elizabeth Lesser
    - Atlas of the Heart by Brené Brown
    - It's OK That You're Not OK by Megan Devine
    - Grief Is the Things With Feathers by Max Porter
    - Notes on Grief by Chimamanda Ngozi Adichie
    - The Wild Edge of Sorrow by Frances Weller
    - Permission to Mourn: A New Way to Grieve by Tom Zuba

- ❏ Sacred Celebrations: Designing Rituals to Navigate Life's Milestone Transitions by Elizabeth Barbour
- ❏ The Geography of Loss by Patti Digh
- ❏ The Grief Recovery Handbook by John James and Russell Friedman
- ❏ Surviving Sibling Loss by Dawn DiRaimondo, PsyD
- ❏ Passed and Present by Alison Gilbert

○ For Students or Professionals

- ❏ Living Through Loss. Interventions Across the Life Span by Hooyman and Kramer
- ❏ The Body Keeps the Score: Brain, Mind, and Body in the Healing of Trauma by Bessel van der Kolk M.D.

○ Poetry

- ❏ <u>If Hearts Had Training Wheels: A Poetry Collection</u> by Ellen Everett
- ❏ The Tears That Taught Me by Morgan Richard Olivier

○ For Children

- ❏ I Miss You: A First Look At Death by Pat Thomas
- ❏ The Invisible String by Patrice Karst
- ❏ Why Do I Feel Sad? By Tracy Lambert LPC
- ❏ The Memory Box: A Book About Grief by Joanna Rowland
- ❏ I'll Always Love You by Hans Wilhelm
- ❏ Wherever You Are My Love Will Find You by Nancy Tillman
- ❏ The Goodbye Book by Todd Parr
- ❏ Nana Upstairs & Nana Downstairs by Tomie dePaola
- ❏ The Fall of Freddie the Leaf by Leo Buscaglia

- Videos
  - https://www.youtube.com/watch?v=khkJkR-ipfw (contains humor)
  - For Children
    - https://dptv.pbslearningmedia.org/resource/grief-media -gallery/sesame-street-in-communities/

## Podcasts

- Where's the Grief by Jordon Ferber
- The Surviving Sibling Podcast by Maya Roffler
- Open to Hope - https://www.opentohope.com/

## Peer Support Groups

- Peer Support Group for Bereaved Siblings - www.siblingisland.com
- The Compassionate Friends for loss of a child, sibling or grandchild - https://www.compassionatefriends.org/
- A Good Goodbye and The Family Plot Blog - https://agood-goodbye.com/
- OneLastWaveProject - instagram @onelastwaveproject

## Support Groups

- Cope Foundation - COPE is a nonprofit grief and healing organization helping parents and families living with the loss of a child. https://copefoundation.org/about/
- NAMI- Mental health organization dedicated to building better lives for the millions of Americans affected by mental illness - https://www.nami.org/
- 988 - Suicide and Crisis Lifeline
- **Helping Parents Heal** - is a non-profit organization dedicated to assisting parents whose children have passed. - https://www.helpingparentsheal.org/

www.ingramcontent.com/pod-product-compliance
Lightning Source LLC
Chambersburg PA
CBHW051304120626
46547CB00015B/2078